IT IS ALL GOOD NEWS!

The Gospel of Jesus Christ That
You May Have Never Heard

Jesse Andrew Harvey

ISBN: 9798357332967

Cover design by: Art Painter
Library of Congress Control Number: 2018675309
Printed in the United States of America

CONTENTS

PREFACE

All scriptures are NKJV unless noted otherwise.

KJV is the King James Version Bible (Public Domain)

NKJV is the New King James Version Bible (Copyright © 1982 by Thomas Nelson. Used by permission.)

TLB is The Living Bible (Copyright © 1971 by Tyndale House Foundation. Used by permission.)

ESV is the English Standard Version Bible (Copyright © 2001 by Crossway. Used by permission.)

YLT is the Young's Literal Translation Bible (Public Domain)

MSG is The MESSAGE Bible (Copyright © 1993, 2002, 2018 by Eugene H. Peterson. Used by permission of NavPress.)

INTRODUCTION

Have you ever looked at a snowflake under a microscope? It is a marvelous creation and to think that each one is unique and different on a molecular level! What a remarkable sight; this tiny droplet of water, frozen ever so carefully by just the right winter conditions and preserved just long enough in the air for us to enjoy.

Our Creator is smart and frankly, that description does not come close to doing Him justice. He designed the snowflake! He figured out how to make each one different! He created the air that transports them! He made us with eyes to see them and even a tongue to stick out in hope of catching just one of these tiny, almost creature-like creations! He even gave us just enough sensory perception to feel one little snowflake touch the tip of our tongue and this same Creator has so much He wants us to discover that it will take more than a lifetime to discover everything; it will take an eternity!

Romans 11:33 tells us, "Oh, the depth of the riches both of the wisdom and knowledge of God" and guess what? It is ALL GOOD NEWS! The Creator of the universe, the God of all the heavens and earth, the Savior of mankind wants you to know this good news today; He wants you to know His unending love; He wants you to have a life that is abundant, free from fear, completely set free like the butterfly who emerges from its cocoon to fly effortlessly over the earth.

The Gospel of Jesus Christ is Good News from God Almighty Himself and is so good that it will radically transform you into something so wonderful, so different that it is as radical a change as becoming a butterfly from a worm! This Good News is so powerful that if you see it and believe it, your life will never be the same! A completely new world will open for you filled with love, that kind of love that all of us search for and long for everyday of our life and the basis of this love is God Himself, as I John 4:8 tells us, "God is love." His very make up is love! He has an infinite amount to give to you and He is longing to give it to you right now!

This Good News is so amazing that only God Himself could be the author of it, the one who created it, and the one who finishes it. The question is do you want this good news for yourself? Do you want this good news to change you so that your life becomes a part of the good news? Do you want this good news to the extent that everywhere you go your life blesses others? Do you want this good news that will bring peace into your life that the Bible describes in Philippians 4:7 as "And the peace of God, which surpasses all comprehension, will guard your hearts and your minds in Christ Jesus"? Do you want this good news that is all about rest for your heart, rest for your emotions, and rest for your soul?

If the answer is yes, read on because you will find that God Himself gave so much to make this happen that in human terms, it is the most sacrificial thing we could do as a parent; to sacrifice our one and only child to save another, "For God so loved the world, that He gave His only Son, that whoever believes in Him should not perish but have eternal life" John 3:16 ESV. That is exactly what He did; He gave His only Son Jesus for you, and this is just in human terms – in "God terms," it is indescribable as to what He really gave in this ultimate sacrifice. What I can tell you is that what He gave us is ALL GOOD NEWS!

IT IS ALL GOOD NEWS
BECAUSE GOD LOVES YOU

**"For God so loved the world
that He gave His only begotten
Son, that whoever believes in
Him should not perish but have
everlasting life." John 3:16**

My first love was in third grade, a blonde-haired girl who wore cat-eye glasses, which was typical in the sixties and that is all I remember about her, but we moved the next year so that was the end of my first "romance." Human love can be fickle that way: here today and gone tomorrow, but God's love is eternal and never changes!

One time I did what I thought was going to be an exhaustive search in the New Testament for all the phrases "God is" but what I found surprised me: there are just three main phrases for God is: God is Love (1 John 4:8), God is Light (1 John 1:5), and God is Spirit (John 4:24) and then the Holy Spirit gave me insight that these fit perfectly with what we believe about God as being one God in three Persons: God the Father (God is Love), God the Son (God is Light) and God the Holy Spirit (God is Spirit).

Is it not amazing that God wants us to know that He is love! God is Love! God the Father's being, and essence wants us to know Him as "love." He has always loved us, and we are the only thing standing in the way of receiving it. He showed us His greatest act of love with the sacrifice of His beloved Son Jesus so that we can live with Him forever – God so loved us that He gave His most valuable possession. Take a moment to think about how valuable and important we are to Him – He first loved us (1 John 4:19) so much that from the very beginning of time, before the foundation of the world, His plan was to give up His one and only Son for us: "the Lamb slain from the foundation of the world" Revelation 13:8.

I have not created or made anything of value except for my children of which there is no amount of money, riches, or treasure that could equate to their worth – they are priceless to me and yes, I made them, with the help of my beautiful wife, of course! In magnificent ways, when we have children, we create them with our God given abilities that let us experience what it is like to be a creator of the most valuable treasure on this earth: our children.

Now, do not get me wrong about our role as "creator." Without God having set everything in motion to have children, this would never be possible; from the wonder of the act of procreation itself, to the awesome dynamics of the 20,000 or so genes that form the human, to the mother who will forever be linked to the child even after the umbilical cord is cut – these are all amazing in and of themselves, but did you know that scientists were able to video the moment conception took place and you know what they observed? Light, they saw a flash of light! This is the moment God did what only He can do: create life. It gives new meaning to the scripture that says, "In Him was life, and the life was the *light* of men" John 1:4.

Not only that but it solidifies what the scriptures say about Jesus: "Then Jesus spoke to them again, saying, 'I am the light of the world. He who follows Me shall not walk in darkness but have the light of life'" John 8:12. Jesus is the light, and "All things were made through Him, and without Him nothing was made that was made" John 1:3. Did you catch that: Jesus is the light, all things are made by Him, and He is the light of men, which tells us He is God who is the creator involved with us in creating offspring!

God participates in every aspect of creation and procreation, even from the beginning of time when Genesis 1:2 tells us, "The Spirit of God moved upon the face of the waters." Yes, the Holy Spirit was there in the beginning and when it came to God creating man, we read in Genesis 1:26, "and God said, let Us make man in Our image, after Our likeness." Did you catch that? It says, "let Us" make man in "Our image" – they all three were there – even the word "God" is plural in the Hebrew: Elohim. The word is "Gods," which is why we say, "God in three persons," as in God the Father, God the Son, and God the Holy Spirit.

I am saying all this because my children, those amazing creations that God blessed me with, can never have a value put on them for which I would say, "Sure, I will take this, or I will take that in exchange for them." Nope, not going to happen and that begs the question, what about the beloved Son of God – is there anything for which God would say, "Sure, you can have my Son in exchange for thus and so."? The amazing answer is YES! There is something God would take in exchange for His one and only Son: YOU! You heard it: He loves you so much that He was willing to give His one and only beloved Son in exchange for you, so that you could spend an eternity with Him and enjoy all the benefits of being His child, forever and ever and that is ALL Good News!

IT IS ALL GOOD NEWS
BECAUSE GOD IS GOOD

**"The goodness of God leads you
to repentance." Romans 2:5b**

When I was a boy there were popular sci-fi TV shows including Lost in Space and Star Trek, which made me think that life existed somewhere in space among all the billions and billions of stars. When I look back to that time in the sixties, it was very unsettling for me with things like the Vietnam War in full swing, nuclear proliferation, the cold war, and the racial divide, even to the point that I would lay on the ground outside, look up to the stars, and say, "I know there is intelligent life out there that is much smarter than we are, so advanced that you can hear me wherever you are. Please, take me with you off this planet and show me your world." Do you know what? Someone did hear me and answer my plea because God is that answer and He is good, desiring to reward anyone who seeks Him. I did not know it at the time but yes, this was my first prayer and God heard me loud and clear!

Do you believe that God is good all the time? If not, how can you trust Him? Yet, it is no surprise that many do not believe He is good all the time saying things like, "If God is so good, tell me why He allows evil to happen?" The question assumes that He does allow evil to happen, but this is not the truth – I will cover this in another chapter.

At this point, it is foundational to our belief that we trust God is good. Not only do we trust He is good, but we expect His goodness to be a part of our life. In church we used to say to each other, "God is good all the time" and then in response the other person would say, "All the time God is good." Now, this may seem like a trivial thing to say but this is good news that we cannot overstate because God is good all the time to me and to you!

Romans 2:4 tells us, "The goodness of God brings us to repentance." The Greek word for goodness means "gentleness and kindness" (as opposed to harsh, hard, sharp, bitter – God is never this way) and specifically applied to God, it means "kind, benevolent – gracious." This is what He is: kind and benevolent to all His creation, gracious to us in every way imaginable and it is to our advantage if we believe this.

Consider Hebrews 11:6b "He who comes to God must believe that He is and that He is a rewarder of those who seek Him" and James 1:17, "Every good gift and every perfect gift is from above and comes down from the Father of lights." If you do not believe God rewards you and gives "every good gift," how can you receive it? His perfect and most complete gift He gave us is Jesus, His beloved Son whom He freely gave to save us so that we can be with Him for eternity – He is a good God!

The New Testament word "repentance" means to "change your mind" so when Romans 2:4 says, "The goodness of God brings us to repentance," this is saying that what changes our mind is the goodness of God. The kindness and benevolence of God is trying to persuade everyone all the time that He loves them and He has only good things for them and that "He is a rewarder of those who seek Him."

When something goes wrong in life, all too often we find ourselves saying, "Why did God do this to me?" or "God is testing me" but nothing could be further from the truth: God is good, always! He is not sending evil our way and He does not test us. Look at what James 1:13 says: "Let no one say when he is tempted, 'I am tempted by God;' for God cannot be tempted by evil, nor does

He Himself tempt anyone." Do you see that? God does not tempt anyone! This word "tempt" in the Greek has the meaning, "to try, make trial of, or to test." This could not be any clearer: God does not test us. He has only good things for us, not evil – God is good all the time.

The New Testament starts with four Gospels. The first is the Gospel According to Matthew. Even though this title is not a part of the original language, the translators decided to add the title so why did they not simply call it the Book of Matthew or the Record of Jesus by Matthew; instead, it is the "Gospel" and this is no accident because this is the very essence of the New Testament: the Gospel, which means "a good message or good news" and that is what these books are: the good news that God gave to us about His beloved Son Jesus because He loves us so much and that is ALL Good News!

IT IS ALL GOOD NEWS BECAUSE GRACE CAME THROUGH JESUS AS A GIFT

"For the law was given through Moses, but grace and truth came through Jesus Christ." John 1:17

My first experience with "Grace," if you will, was watching The George Burns and Gracie Allen Show with my mom and dad. Okay, granted, her name was Gracie, but in my little childlike mind, I always thought of Grace as a person, but when I went to church, they taught that grace is a doctrine or an acrostic such as, "God's Riches At Christ's Expense." What does that even mean? But do you know what? I was not far off in my little childlike thinking because Grace is a person: Jesus.

John 1:17 says, "For the law was given through Moses, but grace and truth came through Jesus Christ." Do you see that? The law was given (it was something given to Moses), but grace and truth came (it was a person who came) – Jesus came; grace and truth came. That is how important to God grace and truth are – He not only sent them in person as a gift, but He did so with His one and only beloved Son Jesus! That is good news!

Now, you may say, "What is the big deal with being sent versus being given?" When I was in my twenties, I received in the mail a "signed" picture of the President of the United States. This was important to me, and it remained framed in my office for years even though the President did not sign it himself (you know, auto-pen signed or something), but I wanted it to be signed by him and therefore it became important to me. However, when the President came to a city nearby, I went to see him. There is just no comparison to the President who was *given* to me in a picture versus the President who *came* to me in person!

For believers, this tells us that grace is not just an impersonal doctrine that we memorize – it is a personal experience with a person who came to give us grace, Jesus, who came to give of Himself to me and to you.

So, what is so special about grace? The answer is one of the most significant reasons why the gospel is all good news. The verse prior to "For the law was given through Moses, but grace and truth came through Jesus Christ," is John 1:16: "For of His fullness we have all received, and grace upon grace" NASB. What is the "grace" for which John says, "For of His fullness we have all received"? Thayer's Greek Lexicon defines grace as "goodwill, loving kindness, or favor" and Strong's Concordance adds: "acceptable, benefit, and gift." Putting it altogether, grace is a gift from God in the person of Jesus where He gives us His favor repeatedly (grace upon grace) as something He wants to do for us, not because we deserve it, not because we earned but because God loves us so much that He sent His one and only beloved Son to give us this free gift of grace. This grace He gives freely comes when God blesses us, heals us, delivers us from fear, provides for us, and saves us from sin and evil. Now, if that is not good news, I do not know what is. In fact, this grace is what brought a revolution into my life so incredible that I began to call myself, "Andy 5.0," (Andy is my nickname used since I was a child) as in version five (5) of Andy Harvey – let me explain.

I heard the gospel message when I was twenty-two at a time when I was searching for something better than my lifestyle offered. I accepted the message and believed in Jesus. This Jesus revolutionized my life, and I have never been the same since. At the time, I could have said, even though I did not think this way, "I am Andy 2.0," as in version two (2) of Andy Harvey – I was changed in such a way by Jesus that I became a new version of myself and that is why the scripture says in 2 Corinthians 5:17, "if anyone is in Christ, he is a new creation; old things have passed away; behold, all things have become new" – I became a new creation, better than just a new version!

Fast forward 25 years when I began to discover the grace of God and once again, I can say it revolutionized my life. I heard preaching that said the number five (5) symbolizes grace and that is when I began to refer to myself as Andy 5.0 (why 5.0 not just 5 – this is an IT thing, as is my professional business background, and it has to do with software versions). Why would I do this? The good news I discovered of grace and the person Jesus who showed me grace, turned my world upside down to the extent that I felt like I was a new version of myself, a version I called 5.0!

The Apostle John presents Jesus to us in such a unique way. Through his gospel, we see Jesus up close and personal, showing us a divine side of what about humanity is important to Him and how He gave of Himself by giving grace everywhere He went. Whether it was His attending a wedding celebration where He did a miracle of luxury by turning water into wine so that all could celebrate this sacred human event or whether it was with the woman at the well, personally interacting with her in a culture where this was forbidden because of traditions made up at the time by religious groups, but He had something more important in mind than human tradition: He wanted to give living water to this woman and her people who were dry and parched from not hearing the true word.

Jesus came to bring grace (undeserved and unearned favor) and everywhere He went He gave Himself away; He gave grace to all He encountered showing us that God is good and wants to bless us with grace upon grace! There was no other way God could show us grace, His favor, in the way He wanted to express it except by sending a person – grace came to us as a person and His name is Jesus!

I must tell you something: I am God's favorite child – did you know that? Well, what is amazing about this is, *so are YOU* His favorite child! Can you grasp that: you are God's favorite child! Do not ask me how He does it, but somehow each one of us is His favorite child. I could not do this with my three children – I would mess it up, but God the Father is able to do this, and His grace makes this most favored status a reality in our lives.

It is wonderful to know that right now, God is thinking about you and saying, "You are my favorite child" and He wants to give you grace upon grace in person through Jesus, each and every day and that is ALL Good News!

IT IS ALL GOOD NEWS BECAUSE JESUS IS THE TRUTH THAT SETS US FREE

"And you shall know the truth, and the truth shall make you free." John 8:32

The first time I thought much about truth was when my mom would let us watch the game show, "To Tell the Truth." You could almost call the show "Who Could Lie the Best" because the show featured a "celebrity" and two other people that were lying to everyone as best as they could to persuade the audience that they were telling the truth when the actual celebrity was the only one telling the truth. Originally, the host was a young Mike Wallace called "A dealer in fact and fiction." It gave me a certain satisfaction being able to guess who was telling the truth but often, the facts presented did not come close to helping me find the celebrity.

John 1:17 says, "For the law was given through Moses, but grace and truth came through Jesus Christ." As I said in the previous chapter, the law was given (it was something given to Moses), but grace and truth came (it was a person who came) – Jesus came, and He brought us truth – He is *the* truth that came. Why is it important that truth came? John 8:32 says, "And you shall know the truth, and the truth shall make you free" and "it was for freedom that Christ set us free" Galatians 5:1 NASU. Jesus did not come to bring us facts – He came to bring us the truth that sets us free.

There is a significant difference between truth and facts – I am talking about the truth as revealed in the person of Jesus Christ and written in the scriptures. Facts are information presented as reality, but they may not be from scripture: biblical truth is eternal, but facts are temporal; biblical truth is absolute, but facts are changing; biblical truth is always true, but facts may not be true. As a believer in Jesus, biblical truth will change your life and set you free.

How does the truth set us free? As an example: You start to feel bad, like you are catching a cold, and you have a bad cough. You decide to search the Internet for what might be wrong – you start to read facts found in the search, and you may begin to wonder if you have something seriously wrong. Not only does this not help you feel better, but now you have all these facts and ideas in your head that may very well be making it worse than it really is!

Taking a different approach, you start reading what is in scripture such as Isaiah 53:5, "by His stripes we are healed" and in 1 Peter 2:24, "who Himself (speaking of Jesus) bore our sins in His own body on the tree, that we, having died to sins, might live for righteousness – by whose stripes you were healed." The Internet gave you facts, but the scriptures gave you truth – as you begin to believe the scriptures, call upon the name of Jesus to heal you saying, "Jesus, by Your stripes I am healed. I want to look to You for healing, not what I read on the Internet. Set me free from all fear so I can believe what Your word says" – now draw near to Him and His word in the scriptures and the truth will begin to make you free of the sickness.

Another example how the truth sets you free: You have a financial situation where you do not have the money to pay your bills. Instead of going down a worrisome path, you decide to read what is in the scriptures: "And my God shall supply all your need according to His riches in glory by Christ Jesus" Philippians 4:19

and "for you know the grace of our Lord Jesus Christ, that though He was rich, yet for your sakes He became poor, that you through His poverty might become rich" 2 Corinthians 8:9. The facts are that you are not sure how you will pay your bills – you can worry about it trying to figure it out on your own or you can call out to Jesus with your need saying, "Jesus, Your word says my God shall supply all my need – I believe Your word and I trust that You will supply all my need." He wants you free of this burden! The truth that sets you free is He wants to supply you with all that you need – trust Him and continue to speak His word, "My God shall supply all my need" and other scriptures until you receive the financial breakthrough for your need.

Jesus said, "You shall know the truth, and the truth shall make you free," and our primary way of knowing the truth is to know Jesus, which is why it was so important that He came. Spend time talking to Him – read about His Life in the Gospels – believe what the scriptures say about Him in Paul's, John's, and Peter's writings and even in the Old Testament. All His promises are "Yes and Amen" designed to make you free and that is ALL Good News!

IT IS ALL GOOD NEWS BECAUSE GOD FORGIVES YOU

"And be kind to one another, tenderhearted, forgiving one another, even as God in Christ forgave you." Ephesians 4:32

I spent my early teenage years in Jacksonville, Florida and let me tell you, it was a dream living there with days spent with my friends doing everything from riding in the sand dunes to surfing on the Florida beaches and I guess I can tell you something since we are way past the statute of limitations: at the age of 14 before I had a license, I drove our families dune buggy on the street to the sand dunes so that I could go trailing for miles with my friends. It was the time of my life!

It was quite devastating for me when my parents told me we had to move from Jacksonville to a small town in Texas because my father's work required him to move. This is the first time I can remember not forgiving someone – I was upset that I had to leave my life in Jacksonville, and it took a long time before I forgave my parents, probably not until after I became a Christian; however, me harboring bitterness and not forgiving them did more harm to me than it did to them.

People like to say, "I can forgive, but I cannot forget." Have you heard that before? Now, in the first place, nowhere in the Bible does God tell you to forgive and then to forget. The devil is adding something (saying you must forget as well) to make forgiveness burdensome. What is interesting and a part of grace is that God is the one who forgets as it says in Hebrews 10:17, "Their sins and their lawless deeds I will remember no more."

God tells us we can forgive others because God in Christ has forgiven us a debt that we were not able to pay and when we forgive, we do ourselves a favor because harboring unforgiveness can lead to bitterness, which will be detrimental to our health! You may ask, "How can I forgive when they do not deserve to be forgiven?"

When you forgive someone, you are not in any way declaring that person deserves forgiveness, and neither are you saying that person is not wrong for what they did! No, forgiving is about something that happens to you when you forgive, which brings us to the answer of how we can forgive.

The truth that sets you free is that God forgives us, and this empowers us to forgive others. The Greek word for "forgive" means "to send away" and "to let go, give up, a debt (remit), by not demanding it." The first time in the New Testament we see the word "forgive" is when Jesus prayed what we call "The Lord's Prayer": "And forgive us our debts, as we forgive our debtors" Matthew 6:12. Jesus prayed this prayer in response to His disciples asking Him to teach them how to pray.

A debt is something you owe. Taking the meaning of the words forgive and debt, the prayer that Jesus said to pray is to ask God to let go of something you owe in the same way you let go of something someone owes you.

Here is the powerful truth Jesus is telling us with this prayer: just as we need to receive God's forgiveness for something we owe, we are doing ourselves a favor by forgiving someone that owes us, but you may say, "How can that possibly help me?" To forgive is to send what they owe you to God who will take care of it. This will be for your benefit! Send it away in the name of Jesus. Stop demanding payment and send it away to God so you will receive forgiveness or release in your heart and mind from all those things you believe others owe you!

Again, you are not saying to that person, "You deserve to be released from what you owe me." You are not saying, "You are right, and I am wrong." No, instead, you are giving God things that He can make right instead of you trying to make them right.

God is always forgiving us of every offence, of every debt we owe because of the finished work of Jesus on the cross. He paid a debt that He did not owe so that you can be free from a debt that you owe. As you believe in the finished work of Jesus and receive forgiveness from God, He sends away that debt so that it no longer demands from you a payment! He did this for you because He loves you and wants you to live a life free of debt, free of owing anything to anyone. Now, through the grace of God, you can forgive and be free of all debts you owe and of all owed to you and that is ALL Good News!

IT IS ALL GOOD NEWS BECAUSE GOD SEES US RIGHTEOUS

"For if by one man's offence death reigned by one; much more they which receive abundance of grace and of the gift of righteousness shall reign in life by one, Jesus Christ." Romans 5:17 KJV

When I was growing up, there was a singing group called The Righteous Brothers. I thought it was such a strange name for a group. I thought they were ministers who were "righteous" or at least more so than the average person, and then to go to church and hear our minister talk about the churches meaning of righteous, it just did not line up. I mean, they were singing songs like, "You've Lost That Loving Feeling" and "Rock and Roll Heaven" and these did not line up with the minister's explanation of being righteous, which was about doing good works. Trying to put all this together was very confusing for a young boy!

The good news is that being righteous is something Jesus does for us by giving us His righteousness so that we can stand before God and have confidence that He sees us as righteous – let me explain.

Righteousness is a gift that we do not earn. Romans 5:17 says, "For if by one man's offence death reigned by one; much more they which *receive* abundance of grace and of *the gift of righteousness* shall reign in life by one, Jesus Christ." For years, I heard preaching saying that to be righteous in the sight of God, I needed to believe in Jesus AND do good works by living a right life, but the truth that sets you free is that we *receive* righteousness as a gift – we do not earn it, nor do we live rightly to be righteousness in God's eyes. This is how we can be confident that He sees us as righteous, not because of anything we do, but because of what Jesus did in giving us this wonderful gift of His righteousness. When God looks upon us, He sees us as righteous because He sees Jesus righteousness upon us.

Thayer's Greek Lexicon gives the meaning of the Greek word for righteousness as a "condition acceptable to God," and "the state of him who is such as he ought to be." How is it that I am "in a state such as I ought (or intended) to be"? How can that be true when I know not everything in my life is right? As the scriptures say, we are righteous by faith and although God sees us as righteous, this righteousness that He gave us is at work in us to make all things as they are intended to be. In other words, He works in your life to change the things in you that are not as they should be into what they should be! How wonderful is that!

Right after I believed in Jesus, He turned my world upside down and frankly, He needed to because I was not leading a good life. Because of drug use, my thinking was not clear resulting in having impaired speech so much so that when I spoke, I stuttered. After I became a believer, when people started asking me to give testimonies about my salvation, I laughed and said, "me, speak to a large crowd," but guess what God did? He made my speech, "as it ought to be" so that I could give clear and powerful testimonies, even to the extent that the first group I gave a testimony to was 400 high school students! I spoke plainly and the students heard the wonderful things God did for me.

How was this possible? God made me righteous (as I should be) by changing the unrighteousness in me (the impaired speech) into righteousness (speech as it should be) and what did I do to receive this? I trusted in His righteousness to work in me to accomplish this righteous work He wanted me to do, and He was able to do this because I received the abundance of His grace and His gift of righteousness so that I could reign in life (live life as it was intended to be) through Jesus.

In the Old Testament story of Abram, before God changed his name to Abraham, we see God blessing him and declaring him as righteous. Before he had children, when he was 99 years of age, it is fascinating that God changed his name to Abraham, which has the meaning "father of a multitude." Can you imagine what it was like when he would meet people and introduce himself: "Hi, I am 'father of a multitude'" when he had zero children? He did so by faith and trust in what God said, and the righteousness of God saw him as a father of a multitude, even though he had not one child.

How could this be that Abraham was righteous or in a state as he was intended to be even though he was far from it? Romans 4:17b says, "God, who gives life to the dead and calls those things which do not exist as though they did" and Romans 4:22 speaking of Abraham says, "and therefore 'it was accounted to him for righteousness.'" God called him Abraham because that is how God saw him, as a father of a multitude and then pronounced him "righteous" until He worked in him by calling those things (Abraham's children) which did not exist as though they did exist until the children came – God works all things for the good!

He wants to do this for you, to work in you to change things that are not righteous (not as they should be) into righteousness (as they should be) and the truth that sets you free is that even before they are changed or before there is evidence of the change, God sees you as being changed, as being righteous as it said in Romans 4:22, He accounts it to you for righteousness because He calls those things (whatever needs to be changed) that do not exist as though they exist. Only God can do this wonderful work of grace!

Your part is to trust in the Lord to work in you, believe in the finished work of Jesus, and receive the gift of righteousness from Him. When we consider that this is not something we have to earn or work for but is a gift of grace that the person Jesus came to give us so that we can live an abundant life, that is ALL Good News!

IT IS ALL GOOD NEWS BECAUSE YOU ARE ACCEPTED IN THE BELOVED

"To the praise of the glory of His grace, by which He made us accepted in the beloved." Ephesians 1:6

Have you ever put in an application for something and then had to wait to see if you were "Accepted?" Did you know that West Point takes all the new cadets through a rigorous six weeks of basic training that is so intense it long ago earned the nickname "Beast Barracks?" Can you imagine the relief and joy at making it through this training and hearing the words "Accepted" – what a cause for celebration! The ALL-good news for us is that when God looks at us, He says, "Accepted" and better yet He says in Ephesians 1:6, "To the praise of the glory of His grace, by which He made us *Accepted in the Beloved.*"

This is not something you do; this is what God does: "He made" – the truth that sets you free is that this is an act of grace God does for you when you believe in Jesus. I want you to hear these words from God to you: "I accept you, I am for you" – meditate on and say these words to yourself – they can be life-changing. As Romans 8:31 says, "If God is for us, who can be against us?" With the God of this universe accepting you and saying He is for you, there is nothing to fear! All He wants for you is blessings, good things, and a life that is full of favor.

It is interesting that the same word in the Greek translated "He has made us accepted" is used only one other time when the angel Gabriel came to Mary to announce the conception and birth of Jesus: "And having come in, the angel said to her, 'Rejoice, *highly favored one*, the Lord is with you; blessed are you among women'" Luke 1:28. Besides the wonderful announcement and prophecy that the angel gave to Mary, this tells us that the same Greek word translated "He has made us accepted" can also say, "highly favored one." In both cases, this is something God does: He makes you accepted and calls you the highly favored one.

This is good news for anyone that feels rejected. Have you ever read the long genealogy of Jesus in Matthew 1:1-17 – it mentions women as a part the genealogy and what is interesting is that they are not woman you might expect such as Sarah or Rebekah, or Leah or Rachel, wives of the patriarchs of the Old Testament. Instead, they are Tamar and Rahab, morally questionable women, and Ruth, who came from a foreign land not accepted by Israel. The ALL-good news for them is that they were all accepted in the beloved Jesus!

You may ask, "How can this be that He accepts me and favors me?" The same verse in Ephesians 1:6 tells us the way we are accepted and favored is "in the beloved." What is the beloved? It is not what but who: Jesus – He is the beloved. What Jesus did on the cross is a complete and finished work that applies to all who declare that He is Lord and believe God raised Him from the dead. He is God's beloved Son that offers all believers grace that He freely gives, by which He can call us "accepted in the beloved," and "highly favored ones" and that is ALL good news!

IT IS ALL GOOD NEWS
BECAUSE IN CHRIST WE HAVE,
WELL, EVERYTHING

**"Therefore, if anyone is in Christ,
he is a new creation; old things have
passed away; behold, all things have
become new." 2 Corinthians 5:17-18**

When we lived in Jacksonville Florida, our family travelled often to my grandparent's house in Williston. I could not wait to arrive and run into the kitchen pantry to see if my grandmother made my favorite cake, a Hershey Bar Pound cake. My favorite thing to do when we visited was to explore the house looking for treasures. For whatever reason, it was a little daunting going into the back room where no one stayed but it looked as if someone lived there, storing treasures ready for me to explore, one of which was an old cedar chest. It was always in the same place but looking for it and then finding it was only half of the fun – the most exciting part of this great exploration was to open the chest and look to see what was inside!

As believers, we have this great treasure "in Christ" and all we need to do is open the treasure box of scripture to see what this treasure is. The Apostle Paul tells us in Ephesians 1:3, "Blessed be the God and Father of our Lord Jesus Christ, who has blessed us with every spiritual blessing in the heavenly places *in Christ*." Did you get that? He said God blessed us with "every spiritual blessing" as a part of being "in Christ." This does not leave anything out because the Greek definition for "every"means "all, any, every, the whole." We get "the whole" thing *in Christ*, every spiritual blessing! The wonderful thing about this is that all we do to receive every spiritual blessing is to be *in Christ*, and that applies to all believers – God puts all believers *in Christ* as it says in Colossians 3:3: "Your life is hidden with Christ in God."

Another treasure to discover *in Christ* is in Romans 8:1: "Therefore there is now no condemnation for those who are in Christ Jesus" NASU. God has no condemnation, judgment, nor bad thoughts towards us, ever. It is the opposite: God only loves us and thinks good thoughts towards us with plans to bless us, protect us, and be with us forever. See this treasure and receive this treasure as a part of being *in Christ* – it will set you free.

Romans 8:2 says, "For the law of the Spirit of life *in Christ* Jesus has made me free from the law of sin and death." We are set free from the law of sin and death because we have the Spirit of life *in Christ* Jesus who cancelled our debts to the law and nailed them to the cross (see Colossians 2:14). We now have the "law of the Spirit of life" that is always working "life" on our behalf or said another way, the Spirit is daily trying to life us!

The best treasure of all is God's love for you! Romans 8:38-39 says, "For I am persuaded that neither death nor life, nor angels nor principalities nor powers, nor things present nor things to come, nor height nor depth, nor any other created thing, shall be able to separate us from the love of God which is *in Christ* Jesus our Lord." This is our treasure to enjoy – God loves me, God loves you and nothing can take that away and that is ALL Good News!

Addendum Note 1 lists the verses that show what we have "in Christ" – this list makes a great study and will benefit anyone who wants to know more about the great treasure we have as a believer "in Christ."

IT IS ALL GOOD NEWS BECAUSE YOU ARE CHOSEN

"For many are called, but few
***are* chosen." Matthew 22:14**

A company "chose" my wife and I to receive "valuable" gifts if we would attend what we thought would be a brief presentation on a timeshare or a piece of property. However, that is not the way I recall it: the presentation seemed anything but brief, and the gifts were not particularly valuable!

In stark contrast, when God chooses you, this is of immense value, receiving a lifetime of benefits and gifts of such value that nothing can compare with their worth and in case you are wondering, this is good news for you as a believer because God has chosen you!

In Matthew 22:1-14 Jesus tells a parable about the kingdom of heaven comparing it to a king who invited guests to the wedding of his son, but those invited did not want to come to the wedding, so the king decided to invite anyone who was willing to attend. Jesus finished the parable with, "For many are called, but few are chosen." I have heard more than one Bible teacher say that this is a hard passage to explain, and we may never understand the meaning, but nothing could be further from the truth.

Jesus prayed for us that the Father would send a "Helper" after He was gone and He did just that – it says in John 14:26 that the Helper is the Holy Spirit who teaches us all things: "But the Helper, the Holy Spirit, whom the Father will send in My name, He will teach you all things." Therefore, passages like this are not hard to understand because it is not up to us to determine the meaning – the Holy Spirit will teach us all things, including the meaning of this passage. How good is that!

The simple explanation of this passage "for many are called, but few are chosen" and how it applies to believers is the following: The king invited (called) those in his kingdom to the wedding of his son, but few of those in his kingdom accepted the invitation, so, he sent his servants everywhere, into the streets to invite anyone who would accept the invitation to the wedding until the king had the number of guests he desired. Those that accepted the invitation and came to the wedding are those that were "chosen" by the king. We as believers are those that received the invitation from God to believe the message of Jesus and we accepted it, making us chosen by God.

How could it be that God chose us before we even knew there was a calling, an invitation to accept? Could it be the simplest explanation that God is so smart that He knew we would accept the invitation when we heard the message? Yes, it is that simple. God looked into the future and saw who would accept the invitation and chose them, making them the "chosen" to attend the wedding of His Son and so much more.

God gave us an invitation to believe in his beloved Son Jesus to be our Savior and we said YES. Little did we know that His invitation and our accepting it was so much more – He has chosen us and now He is giving us an eternity to discover what He has for us before, during, and after the wedding, the marriage supper of the Lamb, and that is ALL Good News!

Addendum Note 2 provides further discussion and study on the meaning of being chosen, the elect, and predestined. As a side note, this chapter is short to make the point that the meaning of being chosen is simple, as I just explained. However, there is depth to the meaning of it, which is why I provided this addendum that looks at most of the verses that use these words.

IT IS ALL GOOD NEWS BECAUSE JESUS GIVES HIS BELOVED SLEEP AND BETTER YET, HE GIVES US REST

"He gives His beloved sleep" Psalms 127:2b and "Come to Me, all you who labor and are heavy laden, and I will give you rest." Matthew 11:28

It is always amazing to me when I ask new parents, "How is the newborn sleeping?" Most parents respond with, "She sleeps all night long!" This was not the case with our children – it turns out that our newborn children did not like to sleep through the night and in fact, one of them did not consistently sleep through the night until he was five years old!

I remember waking up in a daze at about 9 o'clock one Saturday morning thinking that something did not feel right. It took me a while to determine that he did not wake us up early, as he liked to do, and it bothered me so much that when I finally came to my senses, I jumped out of bed and ran into his room to see if he was all right. Of course, he was fine, playing in his room. He mostly slept through the night after that and so did I!

Psalms 127:2 says, "It is vain for you to rise up early, to sit up late, to eat the bread of sorrows; for so He gives His beloved sleep."

You are God's beloved, and this scripture makes it clear that as His beloved, He gives you sleep. If you have trouble sleeping at night, speak out this scripture, meditate upon it, and know that God wants you to sleep – know that as you lie there in bed, He is thinking about you, His beloved and His desire is for you to sleep and to sleep well.

Another meaning to this scripture is, "He gives His beloved *in* sleep." Do you see the difference? He not only gives us sleep but while we are sleeping, He gives to us "in" that time we are sleeping. If you have ever had children, it is when they are sleeping you are able to do things for them such as wash their clothes, make them lunch for school, clean the house and make it safe for them, and pray for them – all while they are sleeping, and how much more God gives to us, even while we are sleeping!

James 1:17 says, "Every good gift and every perfect gift is from above, and comes down from the Father of lights, with whom there is no variation or shadow of turning." God the Father wants to bring gifts, good and perfect gifts to you while you are awake and while you are sleeping. This is grace; this is who He is, and He wants you to know and believe that He gives His beloved sleep, and He gives to His beloved while you are sleeping.

It is all good news to know that Jesus gives us sleep and even better than sleep, He gives us rest! Sleep is good but restful sleep is better. You may fall asleep for a while, but if you are tossing and turning with worry or fear, that sleep will not benefit you like a sleep where your heart and soul are at rest.

When looking at scripture, there is, a principle called the "law of first mention" that tells us that the first time we see a word in the scripture, pay attention to it because it gives us specific keys for understanding that word and lays a foundation for its meaning. The first time we see the word "rest" in the New Testament is in Matthew 11:28-30: "Come to Me, all you who labor and are heavy laden, and I will give you rest. Take My yoke upon you and learn from Me, for I am gentle and lowly in heart, and you will find rest for your souls. For My yoke is easy and My burden is light."

Jesus made it clear that He wants to give us rest and how do we get this rest? "Come to Me" is all He says is necessary. When we come to Him, the passage says, "I will give you rest." That is all there is to it! You do not have to fast and pray for hours to get this rest; you do not have to do ten acts of kindness to get this rest; you do not have to confess your sin to get this rest! Come to Me… and I will give you rest!

This is such a contrast from what the religious leaders of Jesus day put on the people: they had hundreds of laws beyond the scripture that they made a requirement, but Jesus wants you to know, "My yoke is easy, and My burden is light."

Genesis 6:8 gives another important meaning to the word rest: "But Noah found grace in the eyes of the Lord." The Hebrew name Noah has the meaning of "rest" – another way to say this passage is, "But Rest found grace in the eyes of the Lord." Rest is a work of grace – recall that grace is favor from the Lord and the person of Jesus is full of grace that He gives to us, and this includes the gift of rest.

There is a story told in Mark 4:35-41 where Jesus tells the disciples, "Let us cross over to the other side," and they did just that by getting into a boat, and sailing across the Sea of Galilee, but a huge storm came while they were sailing, and you know what Jesus was doing? He was sleeping, even to the point that the storm did not wake Him. Now, when He said, "Let us cross over," you know that He was certain that they would make it to the other side regardless, right? Do you think there was any possibility of them sinking with Jesus in the boat? In fact, He was so confident that He was sleeping, a restful sleep at that but not His disciples who felt like they had to wake Him, thinking they were going to drown but really? If Jesus was sleeping, completely at rest during the storm, then that is the place where He says you can be during the storm: at rest, knowing He has it under control.

You can always rest assured that if He says to you, "Let us cross over," it is not just you but "us" – you and Jesus. Life brings changes and as a believer, Jesus is in our boat – He never leaves us as it says in Hebrews 13:5b-6: "For He Himself has said, 'I will never leave you nor forsake you.' So, we may boldly say: 'The Lord is my helper; I will not fear. What can man do to me?'" It also says in Romans 8:31, "What shall we then say to these things? If God be for us, who can be against us?" KJV.

The Message version of the Bible gives a very descriptive and beautiful meaning to Matthew 11:28-30: "Are you tired? Worn out? Burned out on religion? Come to me. Get away with me and you will recover your life. I will show you how to take a real rest. Walk with me and work with me — watch how I do it. Learn the unforced rhythms of grace. I will not lay anything heavy or ill-fitting on you. Keep company with me and you'll learn to live freely and lightly" MSG.

Only religion has heavy burdens to lay on us but Jesus wants to give you rest from your worries and anxiety, rest from your fears, and rest from all the burdens of your life so that you can be like Him when there is a great storm of life all around you: your heart is resting in the confidence that He is with you, He is for you, and that as you come to Him, He will give you rest and that is ALL Good News!

IT IS ALL GOOD NEWS
BECAUSE GOD CARES

**"Casting all your care upon Him,
for He cares for you." 1 Peter 5:7**

It all begins with believing God is good because God is love (1 John 4:8), and He shows His love in that He cares. Think about that: God cares, He cares for you! He cares for everything you care about – He cares for those you love – He cares for you personally and nothing you do changes that love and care He has for you!

In 1 Peter 5:7 the meaning of the Greek word used for "casting" reminds me of a game we played as children called "Hot Potato" where a group of people stand in a circle and when the music is played, you quickly toss the "hot potato" to someone in the circle until the music stops and the one left holding it is out of the game. The point is to get rid of the hot potato as soon as possible without taking time to think about it because you do not want to be the last one holding it – that is the meaning of casting: to quickly throw something to another.

This is what the Lord is asking us to do: cast or throw any care we have as quickly as possible to Him without giving it a thought and to do it as often as we need to so that we do not keep on caring or worrying about it. He knows the longer we hold on to something, we think about it, our minds churn on it (what about this and what about that and if only this or if only that) like the hamster on the wheel until we have a headache, become anxious, or any one of a hundred different things.

This is an offer to send ALL cares to Him, to throw all things burdening you upon Him because He cares about what you care about, and He can take care of it.

In the same scripture, looking at the Greek meaning for "upon," it has the idea of rest – you cast the care upon the Lord, as often as needed, until your heart and mind are at rest, without anxiety, free of the burdens of the care.

When it comes to rest, Jesus said in Matthew 11:28-30, "Come to Me, all you who labor and are heavy laden, and I will give you rest." This is what we can do: cast the care upon God and rest, knowing He will take care of it.

There is a saying that goes like this: When we rest, God works and when we work, He rests. The meaning is simple: let go of that care by casting it on the Lord and He will do the work that needs to be done to fix, heal, bring us or someone back to the right path, save, and/or finish what He began, all because we take an attitude of rest as we trust Him with the care.

He has got this, and our role is to cast these cares and concerns on Him, repeatedly as necessary, until we can rest in His faithfulness knowing that He will handle that care and if it is a person, when we cast that person upon the Lord, this allows Him to save them and provide peace for us in the midst of the cares and concerns we are so prone to want to carry and that is ALL Good News!

Addendum Note 3 provides further discussion on how God cares for us and insight into why we can cast our cares upon Him.

IT IS ALL GOOD NEWS BECAUSE WE HAVE PEACE WITH GOD

"Therefore, having been justified by faith, we have peace with God through our Lord Jesus Christ." Romans 5:1

I grew up as a teenager in the late sixties and early seventies and one of the popular symbols we would flash is two fingers to represent peace, even saying to one another, "Peace man!" It was more of a gesture during those tumultuous times, with the hope that it would somehow bring peace to our country of which we were in great need. At the time, you could even see President Nixon displaying this gesture of peace when he spoke to crowds. However, it did little for the country and it did not bring the real peace that we need: peace with God and peace in our hearts and minds that comes from God alone through Jesus.

Years ago, I saw a curious picture labeled "Peace" that was a rocky, jagged mountain side, dark with rain pounding the rocks and lightning striking the top. It did not look like peace at all until I looked closely where a bird was asleep in its nest on a jaggy cliff of a rock during the storm – this is a picture of how we can be when we are at peace with God and at peace within our hearts and minds.

Look at Jesus in the story of Mark 4:35-41. The disciples were taking Jesus in a boat to the other side of the Sea of Galilee. As they were sailing, a great storm came upon them and where was Jesus? He was asleep: Mark 4:38 says, "But He was in the stern, asleep on a pillow." Do you think he was worried about not making it to the other side? Was His heart troubled or His mind going crazy with, "What if we had never made this journey?" or "If only we had stayed home?" No, He was in perfect peace, a peace that comes from God alone.

How do we get this kind of peace? It comes from Jesus! He said in John 14:27-28, "Peace I leave with you, My peace I give to you; not as the world gives do I give to you. Let not your heart be troubled, neither let it be afraid." This is a promise on which every believer in Jesus can count! Jesus does not want you to be troubled and He does not want you to be afraid.

Romans 5:1-2 says, "Therefore, having been justified by faith, we have peace with God through our Lord Jesus Christ." As a believer, you have peace with God through Jesus! God is not mad at you! He wants you to know beyond any shadow of doubt that He has forgiven all your sins – there is nothing between you and God: no sin, no shame, and no condemnation! "What then shall we say to these things? If God is for us, who can be against us?" Romans 8:31. God Almighty, Maker and Ruler of the heavens and the earth, is for you! And if God is for you, who can be against you?

You may ask, "How can this be?" The answer is that Jesus took upon Himself all your sins at the cross; He took upon Himself all of God's wrath and judgment against all your sins, past, present, and future, so that you can know God has forgiven you and have eternal peace with Him.

How do I experience this peace every day, moment by moment? Ephesians 2:14 says, "For He Himself is our peace" and Isaiah 26:3 says, "You will keep him in perfect peace, whose mind is stayed on You, because he trusts in You." Our part is to keep our "mind stayed" upon Jesus, trust Him, and He does the rest: He will keep us in "perfect peace."

How do we keep our mind stayed upon Jesus? Philippians 4:6-7 says, "Be anxious for nothing, but in everything by prayer and supplication, with thanksgiving, let your requests be made known to God and the peace of God, which surpasses all understanding, will guard your hearts and minds through Christ Jesus." Prayer can help us keep our focus on Jesus – talk to Him about everything, all the time and the peace of God will do the rest.

Reading the Bible and listening to messages about Jesus is helpful for keeping your mind stayed on Him – meditate on the scriptures and ask the Holy Spirit to show you Jesus in everything you read. The more you think on Jesus and keep your mind focused on Him, God will keep you in peace.

I remember hearing when I was younger that "you are what you eat." For us as believers, it is important to "eat" the right things by thinking on good things, all the time. Philippians 4:8-9 says, "Finally, brethren, whatever things are true, whatever things are noble, whatever things are just, whatever things are pure, whatever things are lovely, whatever things are of good report, if there is any virtue and if there is anything praiseworthy – meditate on these things. The things which you learned, received, and heard and saw in me, these do, and the God of peace will be with you."

This is another key as to how we stay in a state of peace with God, others, and ourselves: meditate on all things good, which can be anything from a beautiful flower to a lovely mountain side or a sandy beach, to the most wonderful gift of all, Jesus, who gave Himself so that we can have peace with God, a peace that goes way beyond understanding and that is ALL Good News!

IT IS ALL GOOD NEWS BECAUSE GOD DOES NOT WANT US TO FEAR

"There is no fear in love; but perfect love casts out fear because fear involves torment. But he who fears has not been made perfect in love." 1 John 4:18

When I was young, I was a boy scout. My dad did scouts with me as one of the leaders. Scouting was a wonderful experience that provided me with helpful life lessons and stories to tell. One yearly event was a scout trip to Billy's island in the Okefenokee Swamp – the only way to get to the island was by boat down a narrow bed of swamp water. There were many reasons to be scared, not the least of which were the alligators, bears, and snakes, all of which we always saw on the trip, but one of scariest parts was all the tales we heard about Billy's island where we stayed, how it was supposed to be a "haunted island." However, all that paled in comparison to the stories the older scouts would tell to try to scare us. The good news for me is that I was never afraid because my dad was with me – with him there, I knew he would not let harm come to me and only wanted good for me. I knew everything was fine!

When Adam and Eve ate from the tree of the knowledge of good and evil, the first sin they experienced was condemnation that led to fear, to be afraid and worse, they were afraid of God – this is always the intent of the devil, to make you afraid of God because if you are afraid of someone, you do not expect good from them, but instead, you expect bad or hurt from them or even to receive condemnation and judgment.

1 John 4:18-19 says, "We need have no fear of someone who loves us perfectly; His perfect love for us eliminates all dread of what He might do to us. If we are afraid, it is for fear of what He might do to us and shows that we are not fully convinced that He really loves us. So, you see, our love for Him comes because of His loving us first" TLB. If we are afraid of God, we wonder what He might do to us such as bring something bad into our lives "to teach us a lesson" or condemn us because He is angry but that could not be further from the truth.

Being afraid of God is a lie from the devil that says, "You cannot trust God to be good" and according to I John 4:18 it is because we do not believe God loves us. The truth that sets you free is that God is love – He is the personification and essence of love. 1 Corinthians 13:4-6 tells us, "Love is very patient and kind, never jealous or envious, never boastful, or proud, never haughty, or selfish or rude. Love does not demand its own way. It is not irritable or touchy. It does not hold grudges and will hardly even notice when others do it wrong" TLB.

The fruit of fear is unbelief or a lack of trust – if you are in any way afraid of God, you will not be able to trust or believe Him for good things and in fact, these two together, fear and unbelief will lead to destructive behavior. According to 1 John 4:18, God's perfect love is the cure to fear: when you know that someone loves you perfectly like He does, you can trust Him to do good in your life, all the time.

It is essential to our well being to believe that God is good, and we can trust Him! This is the foundation for you to be able to trust Him to bring good into your life. Otherwise, you might conclude that if something bad happens, God may have allowed it or worse, caused it to happen.

Instead, as it says in James 1:17-18, "Every good gift and every perfect gift is from above, and comes down from the Father of lights, with whom there is no variation or shadow of turning." God the Father in Heaven is the Father of lights (nothing dark or scary about Him) and it is from Him that every good gift comes to us! He has no "shadow of turning" – He is always the same, always giving good and perfect gifts to us.

The grace revolution that began in my life came as I believed this truth that set me free: God is good all the time and if something bad or evil happens to me, it is not God trying to teach me a lesson, so, there must be someone or something else at work doing this bad. Sometimes it is as the movie character Forrest Gump said, "Stupid is as stupid does," meaning that the bad that is happening right now may be a result of my "stupid does," but there is another cause at work.

One of the greatest insights into scripture that God gave me is that the first three chapters of the Bible (Genesis 1-3) and the last three chapters of the Bible (Revelation 20-22) tell a nearly complete story of how this life on earth began for humanity and how it will end or better yet, how the earth will end as we know it and eternity will begin for all believers. What is left between these six chapters in the Bible is the story of Jesus saving humanity and preparing us for eternity, which is why looking in the first three chapters to see what He is saving us from, gives us great insight into where this fear and evil started for us.

Genesis 3:1 says, "Now the serpent was more cunning than any beast of the field which the Lord God had made. And he said to the woman, has God indeed said, 'You shall not eat of every tree of the garden'?" This passage introduces us to the enemy of God, called the serpent here and in other passages, the devil whose name is Satan. The first words he spoke to them, "has God indeed said," gives us insight that he wants us to doubt everything God says. Let us be clear: Adam and Eve were living in a paradise of good gifts from God, a place where God Himself walked and talked with them, a place free of all disease, hunger, fear, and death, a place where no harm could come to them, and here is the devil asking them to doubt the goodness of God.

Is it no different for us today: the same serpent does not want you to believe God is good all the time, but instead, he wants you to doubt God is good so he lies to you in every way he possibly can with the goal to cast some doubt, lead you to unbelief, and that you need to be afraid of what God might do you, but do not believe anything he says! He is a liar and the father of lies (John 8:44).

As believers, we base what we believe on the scriptures, and they tell us that God is good all the time and He does not want us to be afraid of Him because He loves us perfectly, completely. If you believe this, it will begin a grace revolution in you as it did in me with the result that grace, God's favor, will be yours every single moment of every single day, bringing good and perfect gifts from a good God and that is ALL Good News!

IT IS ALL GOOD NEWS BECAUSE GOD IS WORKING GOOD ON YOUR BEHALF

"In Him also we have obtained an inheritance, being predestined according to the purpose of Him who works all things according to the counsel of His will, that we who first trusted in Christ should be to the praise of His glory." Ephesians 1:11-12

Okay so I was not the best child when it came to the suspense of what each of those beautifully wrapped boxes contained under the Christmas tree, which became evident as I found myself being bold enough to unwrap my presents to find out what was inside because I just could not wait! That is where I learned how to be a good present wrapper or do I say, "re-wrapper." In any case, I just could not wait to see what good gifts my parents gave me because everyone likes gifts!

One thing I hear when it comes to the goodness of God is, "If God is always good, why does He allow evil to happen?" I have heard Bible teachers say that this is a "hard" question that we cannot answer, at least not easily. Their explanation might be something like this: "It is hard to explain the ways of the sovereign Lord, but we just have to trust Him anyway." Now, on the surface this looks like a good response, God is God and He can do what He wants, but if we believe God is good all the time, how do we reconcile that God causes or allows evil to happen such as the massacre of over six million Jews under Nazi Germany? How can we trust Him to always do good – He might just cause or allow something evil to happen to us.

I am here to tell you that God never causes evil to happen to us, nor does He allow evil to happen in the world that humanity so often attributes to Him as being "an act of God." For instance, insurance companies often write into their policies that they may not cover certain "acts of God" such as lightning, floods, or hurricanes, again, sustaining the lie that God causes such tragedies because He allows evil things to happen to us to teach us and discipline us, but nothing could be further from the truth.

All too often, we like to use what happened to Job as the scriptural basis for God testing us and allowing evil to happen to us. We even have a song that quotes what Job said in Job 1:21, "The Lord gave, and the Lord has taken away; blessed be the name of the Lord." This looks truthful on the surface, but it is once again saying God did the evil to Job and his family or at the very least, He allowed the devil to do it.

This belief that God wanted to test Job is based on Job 1:8 where it is all too often taught that God wanted Satan to consider Job for testing because he was strong in his faith, but the Hebrew language does not say that; instead, it is question from God to Satan: Job 1:8a, Young's Literal Translations (YLT) says, "Hast thou set thy heart against My servant Job?" Did you see that? God was not allowing Satan to hurt Job to teach him a lesson or to mature him, as some would say; instead, He is telling Satan, I know what you are going to do, and I know how you are going to do it – God was in no way giving Satan permission to test or harm Job nor his family.

The sad thing is what Job believed: he was afraid all this evil would come upon him, as it says in Job 3:25-26, "For the thing I greatly feared has come upon me and what I dreaded has happened to me. I am not at ease, nor am I quiet; I have no rest, for trouble comes." God knew how the devil was able to harm Job: "The thing I greatly feared has come upon me and what I dreaded has happened to me." Job did not trust God for good and instead, he was afraid and believed evil would come upon him.

Without getting into all the particulars of the Hebrew language and why most translators use this passage to say God allowed the devil to test and ultimately hurt Job (it does not say that), it is the devil being the devil where he plans to harm Job and God telling him not do so but does the devil listen to God? No, he does not; instead, he hurts Job tremendously; however, at the end of the book, in the last chapter, Job acknowledges in Job 42:3-5 that he was wrong about all he was thinking. He now knows that God is good and does not bring harm on him nor his family.

From a human perspective, would you ever allow or give permission to anyone to harm your children? As a good parent, would you ever allow or give permission to them to touch the burning hot stove because "that will teach them a lesson." No, you would not! Would you ever give anyone permission to bring harm to any loved one? Of course, not, and therefore, why would you ever believe that God, who is good all the time, would allow someone to bring harm to His loved ones or do harm to them to teach them a lesson? Frankly, just from a human perspective, it seems absurd. Much more so from a God perspective who demonstrated how He loves us by giving His beloved Son for us – how could we ever believe He would cause evil to come upon us or send bad things to teach us a lesson?

At this point, I hope you now believe in the truth that God does not cause or give permission to anyone to bring harm upon His loved ones. The truth that sets your free is that it is exactly the opposite: He is always working to bring good into your life. Ephesians 1:11 says, "In Him also we have obtained an inheritance, being predestined according to the purpose of Him who works all things." Do you see that: He works all things! In the same verse it says, "In Him also we have obtained an inheritance" – you have a part in everything He owns, and the scripture makes it clear that what we see now with our natural eyes is only a shadow of what is to come.

God is at work on your behalf because He is good and because the good news of the grace of the Lord Jesus is bringing favor and blessing on you all the time. He loves to give good and perfect gifts to His children, and He is doing so as a part of the inheritance that is ours as a believer. He is giving us all things pertaining to life and godliness by supplying all our need according to His riches.

Hebrews 13:20-21 is a great summation of all that God is doing to work good in our lives, not bad: "Now may the God of peace who brought up our Lord Jesus from the dead, that great Shepherd of the sheep, through the blood of the everlasting covenant, make you complete in every good work to do His will, working in you what is well pleasing in His sight, through Jesus Christ, to whom be glory forever and ever. Amen" and that is ALL Good News!

Addendum Note 4 provides further discussion on this topic of why evil happens to people.

IT IS ALL GOOD NEWS BECAUSE GOD SENDS HIS ANGELS TO WATCH OVER US

"For He shall give His angels charge over you to keep you in all your ways." Psalms 91:11

I have been in more than one situation where the Lord sent His angels to protect and bless me and my family. Psalms 91 tells us how the Lord provides protection for us. One way is that He gives His angels "charge" over us to keep us safe wherever we go in life. The Hebrew word "charge" means "to command or commission." God knows when we need help, and He commands His angels to do what is necessary to keep us in all our ways. The Hebrew translation for this verse can be as follows: God commands His angels to guard and protect your course of life. No matter what life brings in your path, God is attentive to it and makes certain you have a path to fulfill your life, free from harm with the intention to bless you and He does so by commanding His angels to watch over you as you go about your life. In other words, their job is to get you to where you are supposed to go and keep you from harm along the way.

The rivers in Texas are known for their water activities including tubing, rafting, diving, and snorkeling. When I was in my twenties, before I was married, I went with a group of friends to snorkel in a river known for its rapids and waterfalls. The person leading the group was a bit on the crazy side, leading all of us right up to the edge of a waterfall, and in fact, it was too close to the edge, at least for me – I went over the waterfall! Obviously, I survived but the rest of the story is that there must have been angels watching over me because down the falls were jagged rocks and at the bottom where the water fell into the plunge-pool, there were large rocks. Not only did I survive but somehow, I managed to go down the rock face of the falls without injury and land in the plunge-pool without harm. Afterwards, my friends tell me I rolled down the fall like a ball. I was quite a sight to see because the rock face of the waterfall had green algae on it, and when I got out of the water my body was green! I know the Lord sent His angels to deliver me and keep me from harm – I have no other explanation how I could have survived without a scratch!

Another experience not as dramatic but equally important happened shortly after I was married. I gave my wife a necklace for our one-year anniversary. While we were shopping, I was on another aisle in the store when I looked to see where my wife was. I could not help but notice her frantic face. I walked quickly to her and asked, "What is wrong?" She said, "I cannot find my necklace." We began to desperately look for it and then a young-looking man walked up to her, opened his hand, and there it was! After she took the necklace from his hand, without a word, he was gone. I am convinced that God sent an angel to help my wife recover something valuable to her and God cares so much for everything in our lives that He made sure she found it!

I encourage you to regularly read Psalms 91. This psalm, more than any other, promises us protection from harm, disease, weapons, and people that use them, plagues, terrors (terrorists), and other bad things that are in life – to sum it up: God protects us from every evil of man and devil!

This protection begins with Psalms 91:1: "He who dwells in the secret place of the Most High shall abide under the shadow of the Almighty." The "he" in this verse is each of us and "the secret place of the Most High" is Jesus (see Colossians 3:3) – that person hidden in Jesus "shall abide under the shadow of the Almighty." You may have heard something like this: "He lives in the shadow of his brother." Often this is a negative quote but for us, this is a good thing, to be under the shadow of the Almighty – do you think anyone, or anything can touch you while you are there? There is no way that is going to happen while you are under His shadow so stay there.

You may ask, "How can I stay there?" The verse says, "He who dwells" – to "dwell" in the Hebrew means "to sit down." God has no interest to make this complicated, which is why He makes it as easy as sitting down – this is a reference to rest, something I spoke about in a previous chapter. Jesus made it clear that He wants to give us rest and how do we get this rest? Jesus said, "Come to me… and I will give you rest." To receive Psalms 91 protection, come to Jesus and He will give you rest so that you can sit down and stop fighting on your own. The result is that the Lord hides you from anyone and anything trying to fight against you.

God's desire is to protect us; He wants to protect you and He wants to protect me! I encourage you to make Psalms 91 a regular part of your prayer life by praying the scripture. For instance, I pray like this using Psalms 91: "He who is resting – that is me Lord – in the secret place of the most High – that is You Jesus – is constantly staying under the shadow of the Almighty – God, I am quite happy to live under your shadow of protection from all evil and harm." Whatever works for you, Psalms 91 makes a promise that God protects you and considering that God has a myriad of angels to watch over you all the time, that is ALL Good News!

IT IS ALL GOOD NEWS BECAUSE JESUS WILL RETURN TO BRING US HOME

"For the Lord Himself will descend from heaven with a shout, with the voice of an archangel, and with the trumpet of God. And the dead in Christ will rise first. Then we who are alive and remain shall be caught up together with them in the clouds to meet the Lord in the air. And thus, we shall always be with the Lord. Therefore comfort one another with these words." Romans 8:31

I once heard someone say, "You know if you ask a theologian about the return of Jesus, you might get a dissertation on the dispensations of the end times complete with explanations on the meaning of the rapture and the judgment of God, but if you ask a new believer or a child about the return of Jesus, they may just look to the skies and say, 'Where? Is He coming now?'"

That must be why Jesus said in Matthew 18:3, "Assuredly, I say to you, unless you are converted and become as little children, you will by no means enter the kingdom of heaven." Children are simple and believe easier than adults, taking at face value what is said, which brings me to another scripture in 2 Corinthians 11:3 where the Apostle Paul was concerned for the believer saying, "But I fear, lest somehow, as the serpent deceived Eve by his craftiness, so your minds may be corrupted from the simplicity that is in Christ." We often make it too complicated when all along, God wants us to be like a child in the way we believe and even think by accepting what He says, just like He said it.

And so, it is with the return of Jesus and how we think about it: Where? Is He coming now? This is ALL-good news for all who believe in Jesus. Just look at scriptures about his return: 1 Corinthians 15:51-53 says, "Behold, I tell you a mystery: We shall not all sleep, but we shall all be changed – in a moment, in the twinkling of an eye, at the last trumpet. For the trumpet will sound, and the dead will be raised incorruptible, and we shall be changed."

To live forever, we will receive a new body, one that is incorruptible and immortal, free of disease and fatigue, one that is ageless and strong. Even better, this body will be like the body of Jesus when God resurrected Him from the grave, giving Him wonderful abilities, such as being able to pass through walls and move from one place to another unencumbered by space and time (see 1 John 3:2).

Shortly after we receive our new body, we will reign with Him on the Earth in His kingdom for a thousand years. One of my favorite passages about this is Daniel 7:9-10, 13-14, 27: "I watched till thrones were put in place, and the Ancient of Days was seated; His garment was white as snow, and the hair of His head was like pure wool. His throne was a fiery flame, its wheels a burning fire; a fiery stream issued and came forth from before Him. A thousand-thousands ministered to Him; ten thousand times ten thousand stood before Him. The court was seated, and the books were opened. I was watching in the night visions, and behold, one like the Son of Man, coming with the clouds of heaven! He came to the Ancient of Days, and they brought Him near before Him. Then to Him was given dominion and glory and a kingdom, that all peoples, nations, and languages should serve Him. His dominion is an everlasting dominion, which shall not pass away, and His kingdom the one which shall not be destroyed. Then the kingdom and dominion and the greatness of the kingdoms under the whole heaven shall be given to the people, the saints of the Most High. His kingdom is an everlasting kingdom, and all dominions shall serve and obey Him."

What an exciting time this will be! And the only reason we would find ourselves not being a part is that we have not believed in Jesus. So, what do you think? Will you be a part of this most blessed and exciting event, the return of Jesus, and if not, do you want to be?

I had a vision recently where I was standing with a massive group of believers – we were all standing around the throne of God and talking among ourselves saying, "Hey, there is Moses and Jacob, and there is Paul – that is Isaiah and Zechariah (we all knew in the vision who everybody was) and over there is Billy Graham." It was such an exhilarating time with such joy that words cannot describe it.

The simplicity of how to become a believer in Jesus and then be a part of this exciting future is what it says in Romans 10:9-13: "That if you confess with your mouth the Lord Jesus and believe in your heart that God has raised Him from the dead, you will be saved. For with the heart one believes unto righteousness, and with the mouth confession is made unto salvation. For the Scripture says, 'Whoever believes on Him will not be put to shame.' For there is no distinction between Jew and Greek, for the same Lord over all is rich to all who call upon Him. For 'whoever calls on the name of the Lord shall be saved.'"

That is all there is to it. I hope that if you have not called on the name of the Lord Jesus, you will do so now. You can pray something as simple as this: "Jesus, I believe in who You say You are: You are Lord and Savior. I believe God raised You from the dead. I want to receive everything there is to receive from this ALL-good news gospel. Amen."

All that we have now and all we are looking forward to is beyond description! God the Father loves us and made a way for us to be with Him forever by sending His beloved Son Jesus to die for our sin so that we can live forever as kings and priests. God cares for us infinitely and wants only good for us – He is gracious and kind, wanting us to be at peace and rest, sending His angels to watch over and protect us and He will do everything necessary to ensure we will live forever with Him and our Savior Jesus! Truly, the Gospel of Jesus Christ is ALL good news; in truth, it is **ALL VERY GOOD NEWS**!

ADDENDUM NOTE 1

These are the scripture verses showing what we have "in Christ." As it says in Ephesians 6:17, one of the weapons of our warfare is "the sword of the Spirit, which is the word of God." It is the only offensive weapon we have for fighting the devil and what is it? The word of God, the Bible, the scriptures. Study these verses, meditate upon them, and use them in your fight for the faith to believe and stand firm in the truth that you are in Christ.

Romans 3:24: Being justified freely by His grace through the redemption that is *in Christ* Jesus.

Romans 6:11: Likewise, you also, reckon yourselves to be dead indeed to sin, but alive to God *in Christ* Jesus our Lord.

Romans 6:23: For the wages of sin is death, but the gift of God is eternal life *in Christ* Jesus our Lord.

Romans 8:1: There is therefore now no condemnation to those who are *in Christ* Jesus, who do not walk according to the flesh, but according to the Spirit.

Romans 8:2: For the law of the Spirit of life *in Christ* Jesus has made me free from the law of sin and death.

Romans 8:38-39: For I am persuaded that neither death nor life, nor angels nor principalities nor powers, nor things present nor things to come, nor height nor depth, nor any other created thing, shall be able to separate us from the love of God which is *in Christ* Jesus our Lord.

1 Corinthians 1:2: To the church of God, which is at Corinth, to those who are sanctified *in Christ* Jesus, called to be saints, with all who in every place call on the name of Jesus Christ our Lord, both theirs and ours.

1 Corinthians 1:30: But of Him you are *in Christ* Jesus, who became for us wisdom from God — and righteousness, sanctification, and redemption.

1 Corinthians 4:10: We are fools for Christ's sake, but you are wise *in Christ*! We are weak, but you are strong! You are distinguished, but we are dishonored!

1 Corinthians 4:15: For though you might have ten thousand instructors *in Christ*, yet you do not have many fathers; for *in Christ* Jesus, I have begotten you through the gospel.

1 Corinthians 15:19: If in this life only we have hope *in Christ*, we are of all men the most pitiable.

1 Corinthians 15:22: For as in Adam all die, even so *in Christ* all shall be made alive.

2 Corinthians 1:21: Now He who establishes us with you *in Christ* and has anointed us is God.

2 Corinthians 2:14: Now thanks be to God who always leads us in triumph *in Christ*, and through us diffuses the fragrance of His knowledge in every place.

2 Corinthians 3:14: But their minds were blinded. For until this day the same veil remains un-lifted in the reading of the Old Testament, because the veil is taken away *in Christ*.

2 Corinthians 5:17: Therefore, if anyone is *in Christ*, he is a new creation; old things have passed away; behold, all things have become new.

2 Corinthians 5:19: That is, that God was *in Christ* reconciling the world to Himself, not imputing their trespasses to them, and has committed to us the word of reconciliation.

2 Corinthians 11:3: But I fear, lest somehow, as the serpent deceived Eve by his craftiness, so your minds may be corrupted from the simplicity that is *in Christ*.

Galatians 2:4: And this occurred because of false brethren secretly brought in (who came in by stealth to spy out our liberty which we have *in Christ* Jesus, that they might bring us into bondage).

Galatians 2:16: Knowing that a man is not justified by the works of the law but by faith in Jesus Christ, even we have believed *in Christ* Jesus, that we might be justified by faith *in Christ* and not by the works of the law; for by the works of the law no flesh shall be justified.

Galatians 3:14: That the blessing of Abraham might come upon the Gentiles *in Christ* Jesus, that we might receive the promise of the Spirit through faith.

Galatians 3:26: For you are all sons of God through faith *in Christ* Jesus.

Galatians 3:28: There is neither Jew nor Greek, there is neither slave nor free, there is neither male nor female; for you are all one *in Christ* Jesus.

Ephesians 1:3: Blessed be the God and Father of our Lord Jesus Christ, who has blessed us with every spiritual blessing in the heavenly places *in Christ*.

Ephesians 1:10: That in the dispensation of the fullness of the times He might gather together in one all things *in Christ*, both which are in heaven, and which are on earth in Him.

Ephesians 1:12: That we who first trusted *in Christ* should be to the praise of His glory.

Ephesians 1:15-21: Therefore I also, after I heard of your faith in the Lord Jesus and your love for all the saints, do not cease to give thanks for you, making mention of you in my prayers: that the God of our Lord Jesus Christ, the Father of glory, may give to you the spirit of wisdom and revelation in the knowledge of Him, the eyes of your understanding being enlightened; that you may know what is the hope of His calling, what are the riches of the glory of His inheritance in the saints, and what is the exceeding greatness of His power toward us who believe, according to the working of His mighty power which He worked *in Christ* when He raised Him from the dead and seated Him at His right hand in the heavenly places, far above all principality and power and might and dominion, and every name that is named, not only in this age but also in that which is to come.

Ephesians 2:4-7: But God, who is rich in mercy, because of His great love with which He loved us, even when we were dead in trespasses, made us alive together with Christ (by grace you have been saved), and raised us up together, and made us sit together in the heavenly places *in Christ* Jesus, that in the ages to come He might show the exceeding riches of His grace in His kindness toward us *in Christ* Jesus.

Ephesians 2:10: For we are His workmanship, created *in Christ* Jesus for good works, which God prepared beforehand that we should walk in them.

Ephesians 2:13: But now *in Christ* Jesus you who once were far off have been brought near by the blood of Christ.

Ephesians 3:6: That the Gentiles should be fellow heirs, of the same body, and partakers of His promise *in Christ* through the gospel.

Ephesians 3:11: According to the eternal purpose, which He accomplished *in Christ* Jesus our Lord.

Ephesians 4:32: And be kind to one another, tenderhearted, forgiving one another, even as God *in Christ* forgave you.

Philippians 3:3: For we are the circumcision, who worship God in the Spirit, rejoice *in Christ* Jesus, and have no confidence in the flesh

Philippians 3:9: And be found in Him, not having my own

righteousness, which is from the law, but that which is through faith *in Christ*, the righteousness which is from God by faith.

Philippians 3:14: I press toward the goal for the prize of the upward call of God *in Christ* Jesus.

Colossians 1:19: For it pleased the Father that *in Christ* all the fullness should dwell.

Colossians 1:28: Him we preach, warning every man and teaching every man in all wisdom, that we may present every man perfect *in Christ* Jesus.

1 Thessalonians 4:16: For the Lord Himself will descend from heaven with a shout, with the voice of an archangel, and with the trumpet of God. And the dead *in Christ* will rise first.

1 Thessalonians 5:18: In everything give thanks; for this is the will of God *in Christ* Jesus for you.

1 Timothy 1:14: And the grace of our Lord was exceedingly abundant, with faith and love, which are *in Christ* Jesus.

1 Timothy 3:13: For those who have served well as deacons obtain for themselves a good standing and great boldness in the faith, which is *in Christ* Jesus.

2 Timothy 1:1: Paul, an apostle of Jesus Christ by the will of God, according to the promise of life which is *in Christ* Jesus

2 Timothy 1:9: Who has saved us and called us with a holy calling, not according to our works, but according to His own purpose and grace which was given to us *in Christ* Jesus before time began?

2 Timothy 1:13: Hold fast the pattern of sound words, which you have heard from me, in faith and love which are *in Christ* Jesus.

2 Timothy 2:1: You, therefore, my son, be strong in the grace that is *in Christ* Jesus.

2 Timothy 2:10: Therefore, I endure all things for the sake of the elect, that they also may obtain the salvation, which is *in Christ* Jesus with eternal glory.

2 Timothy 3:12: Yes, and all who desire to live godly *in Christ* Jesus will suffer persecution.

2 Timothy 3:15: And that from childhood you have known the Holy Scriptures, which are able to make you wise for salvation through faith, which is *in Christ* Jesus.

Philemon 6: That the sharing of your faith may become effective by the acknowledgment of every good thing which is in you *in Christ* Jesus.

ADDENDUM NOTE 2

This section provides additional notes on the scriptures that use the words called, chosen, and the elect, as well as the word predestined. This study is not definitive; instead, it is more information to help you understand the simplicity of these words and how to conclude for yourself their meaning. It says in John 14:26 that "the Holy Spirit, whom the Father will send in My name, He will teach you all things." Ask Him to teach you and show you the truth that sets you free.

Matthew 22:1-14 is the only pre-Paul passage where the word "called" is used (Matthew 20:16 has this same language added by TR (see note 1. below) text but it is not in the NU (see note 2. below) text). In the context of this, the "called" (invited) are the wedding guests who were invited to come to the wedding of the king's son – many were invited (called) but few accepted the invitation and even some who did accept it, did not do so properly (i.e., did not have the wedding garment that is given to all those who accept the invitation). This passage distinguishes the "chosen" as those who responded the correct way – they came to the wedding in proper clothing and the invited (called) that "were not worthy" are those that did not respond to the invitation. It is clear from the passage that God is calling many and if they respond, they are "chosen." This story is about the marriage supper of the lamb (Revelation 19:19) where God invited Israel, but they were unwilling to come so He invited the Gentiles. Those who responded by putting on Jesus (Romans 13:14), are those who responded to the call (invitation) and became the chosen by accepting the invitation and attending the wedding.

The passage in Matthew 22:1-14 is a parable with underlying meanings – it is more than just a nice story; it is a story with truth that we can discover as the Holy Spirit teaches us. Romans 13:14 says, "But put on the Lord Jesus Christ, and make no provision for the flesh, to fulfill its lusts." In this passage, the word "put on" in Greek is "Enduo" meaning "to array or clothe with." The same word used in Matthew 22:11 where it says, "not have on" where it adds "not" to "endue" meaning "not clothed with." Letting scripture interpret scripture, the person at the wedding who did not have on the proper wedding clothes, did not have Jesus – he did not accept the invitation that the king gave, in the way the king gave it, and instead, he determined to go the wedding his way.

To summarize the meaning of the passage, Jesus is the Son of the King whose wedding it is. He, along with the King, who is God the Father, are the Ones inviting us to come the wedding. God provides the invitation and the clothes to wear, which is none other than Jesus Himself and when we accept that invitation as God designed it, we become "chosen" and will be with Jesus at the wedding.

Therefore, being "called" is an invitation from God who graciously invites (calls) us to all that He has for humanity, which primarily is to know Jesus and receive all the benefits thereof, but it is a choice, an invitation for which we can say yes or no.

Revelation 17:14 says, "These shall make war with the Lamb, and the Lamb shall overcome them: for He is Lord of lords, and King of kings: and they that are with Him are called, and chosen, and faithful." The "called" will be with Jesus when He makes war against all those that oppose Him, which are the devil and his demons. What makes this interesting is finding the word "called" (Greek word Kletos) and the word "chosen" (Greek word Eklektos) together indicating that they are meant to be complete together, as I have been saying – the literal Greek says, "those with Him are called (or invited) and chosen (or elect) and faithful (or steadfast)."

One might ask why do we see them together in the scriptures? The truth that sets you free is that if you are the chosen, you have been called and you are faithful – they all go together and form a unity or as Ecclesiastes calls it, "a three form chord" that is not easily broken; however, just because you have one, you do not have them all – just as the first scripture said, not all that are called are chosen, but all that are chosen are called and all that are faithful are both chosen and called! What a great salvation!

Are they different? Well, yes, if you get into the details of each word but that will not be discussed here – in this discussion I am wanting to show you the simplicity of what it means to be called and chosen, which we will find is like the other so called "hard" words, election and predestined, but nothing could be further from the truth – they are simple to understand. Paul told us in 2 Corinthians 11:3, "But I fear, lest by any means, as the serpent beguiled Eve through his subtlety, so your minds should be corrupted from the simplicity that is in Christ" – do not be drawn away from the simple explanation if the complex leaves you scratching your head and not able to understand and believe.

The word "chosen" (Eklektos) is the same word translated as "elect" with its definition "to choose, to select as a favorite." Does God really have favorites? What if it is as simple as what I previously said with us being called and chosen resulting in becoming His favorites? Am I saying that I am God's favorite? Yes, I am God's favorite but the truth that sets you free is that so are you if you are a believer! Only God can make every believer not just feel like we are His favorite, but He makes each one of us His favorite!

Thayer's Greek Lexicon gives a simple definition to the word elect as chosen by God, to obtain salvation through Christ. Can it be any simpler? We are chosen, we are favored to obtain salvation through Jesus, and that is the simplicity of it!

Romans 8:33 says, "Who shall lay anything to the charge of God's elect? It is God that justified us." The elect people are those that

God justifies, and the word "justifies" is the word that Thayer's Greek Lexicon defines as "to make, to render righteous or such as he ought to be" – so a justified person is righteous, and this is something God does when we believe (Romans 10:9-10).

2 Timothy 2:10 says, "Therefore I endure all things for the elect's sakes, that they may also obtain the salvation which is in Christ Jesus with eternal glory" and Titus 1:1 says, "Paul, a servant of God, and an apostle of Jesus Christ, according to the faith of God's elect, and the acknowledging of the truth which is after godliness." These are passages where Paul does not distinguish from "regular" believers and the "elect" believers. Why? Because they are one in the same – we are all the elect!

Colossians 3:12 says, "So, as those who have been chosen of God, holy and beloved..." Here Paul references ALL who are in Christ (vs. 11 says there is no distinction between Greek and Jew, circumcised and uncircumcised, barbarian, Scythian, slave and freeman, but Christ is all, and in all) as being "chosen by God" and goes on to say that they are "holy and beloved" – the saints (holy ones) are what we become when we believe, not something we do but something God chose us to be – we believed and He chose that a part of our salvation, of His grace, would be that we become "holy" – what a gracious God! And beloved sounds like that part of chosen that says we are His favorite and the truth that sets you free is that you are His favorite! And so am I! All of us are our Daddy's favorite, only something God can do the right way, fully and completely!

1 Peter 1:1 says, "Peter, an apostle of Jesus Christ, to those who reside as aliens, scattered throughout Pontus, Galatia, Cappadocia, Asia, and Bithynia, who are chosen." Here is another apostle that does not distinguish the "elect or chosen" from all believers and he introduces us to why the scripture calls us "chosen" as if God picked and chose who would be believers: 1 Peter 1:1-2 "who are chosen according to the foreknowledge of God the Father." Now, is this not obvious, that God is so smart, has so much knowledge and

in this case knowledge before an event took place, that He knew that He could choose us because He knew we would respond to the call! We are "chosen" by God because He knew we would respond to the invitation!

In 1 Peter 2:4-9 he carries on the same theme that all believers are "chosen of God" and "a chosen generation" just as Jesus is "elect" and "precious."

Looking at a few other places where "election" is used, it is the same root word used for the elect or chosen and is the overall act of choosing so that when the scripture speaks of election, it is the Holy Spirit speaking of the overall view to those who are the elect, the believers in Jesus.

Romans 9:10-13 says, "There was Rebekah also, when she had conceived twins by one man, our father Isaac; for though the twins were not yet born and had not done anything good or bad, so that God's purpose according to His choice would stand, not because of works but because of Him who calls, it was said to her, 'THE OLDER WILL SERVE THE YOUNGER.' Just as the scripture says, 'JACOB I LOVED, BUT ESAU I HATED.'"

These verses seem harsh and not like the Jesus I know but interpreting the Bible with the Bible, first we know that election and choosing is according to God's foreknowledge – He is smart enough to know the entire picture of Jacob from when he was born to when he became a nation and everything about Esau as well. In looking at this picture, God in his foreknowledge did not like what He saw when He looked at the future of Esau and in fact, He hated it; however, He loved what He saw in the future of Jacob.

What did God see beforehand that He could say, "ESAU I HATED"? He saw everything including that Esau would sell his birthright for a pot of stew, that he would become a bitter man who did not believe in the promises of God, that his descendants and the land of Esau (called Edom) would revolt against the land of Judah, and many prophecies made against Edom that its land would become desolate and laid to waste, never to be inhabited again, which happened and remains to this day. Therefore, in His unfathomable foreknowledge (knowledge of the future) God could say, "ESAU I HATED."

On another note, Romans 9:14ff simply says that if God wants to have mercy on one but not another, that is His prerogative and frankly, who am I to question the smartest, wisest, most insightful (for lack of any adequate words to describe the greatness of God) person (again, for lack of a better word to make this discussion real) that exists on why He has mercy on one but not another. God knows what He is doing, and my faith just needs to say, "Amen!"

Romans 11:5 says, "Even so then at this present time also there is a remnant according to the election of grace." Now, beyond the election of Jacob over Esau, which again is because of God's foreknowledge, there is another election or choosing "by grace" – this is in an analogous way, a choosing by God because of the freely given unmerited, undeserved favor (grace) of God that comes from the finished work of Jesus as Savior of all who confess with their mouth "Lord Jesus" and believe that God raised Jesus from the dead (Romans 10:9-10). This should stop all speculation about God's love and mercy as He has waited (He is waiting for the remnant according to the election of grace) over 2,000 years so that all people, including the remnant of Israel, could receive this free-gift of grace through the Lord Jesus – nothing we do to deserve it, but a simple confession and faith makes us automatically elected.

Romans 11:26-28 says, "And so all Israel shall be saved: as it is written, 'There shall come out of Zion the Deliverer, and shall turn away ungodliness from Jacob: For this is my covenant unto them, when I shall take away their sins.' Concerning the gospel, they are enemies for your sake, but concerning the election they are beloved for the sake of the fathers."

What is this? All of Israel "shall be saved"? It may beg the question, "If God is love, how can He pick and choose?" Does not this statement say that in any case, all of Israel is saved? That is love, mercy, and grace. Therefore, this passage makes clear that because of God's election, His foreknowledge of what Israel will do when "There shall come out of Zion the Deliverer and shall turn away ungodliness from Jacob: For this is my covenant unto them, when I shall take away their sins," they will all turn to the God of Israel, and they shall be saved! What a kind and merciful God!

In 1 Thessalonians 1:4 Paul encourages them to know their election – nothing more than to know but again, not distinguishing between this or that person in Christ because all believers are a part of the election.

2 Peter 1:10 says, "Wherefore the rather, brethren, give diligence to make your calling and election sure: for if you do these things, you shall never fall."

Peter first lumps calling and election together to signify that they go together – if we hear and receive the invitation (the calling), we become the elected. Second, he encourages us to make "sure" the calling and election – this has the idea of being steadfast, firm, or stable.

Hebrews 6:17-20 says, "In the same way God, desiring even more to show to the heirs of the promise the unchangeableness of His purpose, interposed with an oath, so that by two unchangeable things in which it is impossible for God to lie, we who have taken refuge would have strong encouragement to take hold of the hope set before us. This hope we have as an anchor of the soul, a hope both sure and steadfast and one which enters within the veil, where Jesus has entered as a forerunner for us, having become a high priest forever according to the order of Melchizedek."

The author of Hebrews wants us to let this truth of election, of choosing, of God's favor to become an anchor in our hope and faith. Do not believe a Bible teacher that says, "You may not be elected so do (emphasis on works) something to make certain you are a part of the elect." No sir! It is by grace through faith and not of works (Galatians 2:20).

To summarize the meaning of election: the word election comes from the same word as elect where it speaks of the overall view to those who are the elect, the believers in Jesus and again, this is all according to God's foreknowledge (knowledge of the future). Though we see passages that on the surface look hard and cold (Jacob I loved, and Esau I hated), election or choosing are statements with a view to the future because of what God knew even before they were born, thus making it possible to say what God said. And besides all of that, when the election of grace came through the giving of His own Son so that ALL believers could become His favorites, I hope this brings all of us to a place of yes and amen, You are a good God who wants us to understand and believe in the scriptures that say I am chosen and one of the elect because I accepted the invitation, the calling to know Jesus and be a part of the wedding supper of the Lamb of God, slain from the foundation of the world!

One last word to look at is "predestination." Romans 8:29-30 says, "For those whom He foreknew, He also predestined to become conformed to the image of His Son, so that He would be the firstborn among many brethren; and these whom He predestined, He also called; and these whom He called, He also justified; and these whom He justified, He also glorified."

The Greek word "predestined" means "to predetermine, decide beforehand" – what did God decide beforehand? This passage makes it clear without any doubt: "to become conformed to the image of His Son" – this is not complicated and is nothing else but a statement about what God said we would become.

Again, this is all about God's foreknowledge – He is smart enough to know that this is our destiny that we will be like Jesus! Because He knew this would occur, He called us, He sent the invitation, and when we received it, He justified us, and He made us righteous!

Ephesians 1:5-6 says, "He predestined us to adoption as sons through Jesus Christ to Himself, according to the kind intention of His will, to the praise of the glory of His grace, which He freely bestowed on us in the Beloved."

This is another lovely passage about what He would do for us, ALL believers, is to adopt us as sons and daughters! Again, the passage makes it clear that this is by "His grace, which He freely bestowed on us" – it is free and freely given!

Paul continues in Ephesians 1:11-12: "Also we have obtained an inheritance, having been predestined according to His purpose who works all things after the counsel of His will, to the end that we who were the first to hope in Christ would be to the praise of His glory."

We will obtain an inheritance because He predestined us to "be to the praise of His glory." This is all about Him and what He does – He does it all! That is ALL good news!

1 Corinthians 2:7-8 says, "We speak God's wisdom in a mystery, the hidden wisdom which God predestined before the ages to our glory."

This last passage is just telling us that God is smart enough that He could have this "hidden wisdom" and keep it hidden until the right time, almost like a good mystery novel that is actually a real life story of this great plan where God would go to all the trouble to create all this for us, ask us to take care of it and enjoy it fully, and then when we rebelled and messed up, came up with a plan in advance to predestine us to this great salvation, without a single requirement other that we just take the invitation, receive Him, and believe in Him – this is ALL good news!

To summarize this discussion of what it means to be "chosen" or "elect": all believers are "chosen" or the "elect" – as Thayer's Greek Lexicon says, elect is defined as "to choose, to select as a favorite" and 1 Peter 1:1 says this is according to God's foreknowledge so that the choosing is because God knew we would respond to the call, i.e. He is smart enough to know this and the result is we ALL become His favorites or highly favored ones, the very essence of grace.

To summarize the word "predestined," God determined a long time ago, before He created the heavens and the earth that He would adopt believers as His children, made to be like Jesus, given an inheritance, and the result would be that we would all be to the praise of His glory.

Conclusion: This tells a beautiful story of redemption where God determined a long time ago, before He created the heavens and the earth that He would adopt believers as His children, made to be like Jesus, given an inheritance, and the result would be that we would all be to the praise of His glory. To make this happen, He sent His only Son to die for our sin, to take every disease, all poverty, all mental anguish, every human torment so that He could issue a call, an invitation to believe, where if we accepted, we became chosen, the elect, His favored ones, and receive all the benefits of predestination. God is so good and that is ALL Good News!

1. TR - this is the Bible text found in the Textus Receptus. It is the main text used for scriptural translations that form the basis of the King James versions of the Bible including the KJV (King James Version) and the NKJV (New King James Version).

2. NU - this is the Bible text found in the Nestle-Aland Greek New Testament (N) and the United Bible Society's third edition (U). It is the main text used for scriptural translations that form the basis of versions of the Bible including the NASB (New American Standard Version) and the ESV (English Standard Version).

ADDENDUM NOTE 3

This discussion provides additional notes and scriptures from the Old Testament about casting your care on God.

The Hebrew version of "Casting all your care upon Him, for He cares for you" (1 Peter 5:7) is Psalms 55:22 (it may be what Peter was thinking of when he wrote this scripture) that says to "Cast your burden on the Lord."

This verse gives us another sense of how we can do this. The Hebrew alphabet tells us that every letter is a picture, represents a number, and has a meaning. For instance, the first letter Aleph is a picture of a bull, represents the number one (1), and has multiple meanings including that of a sacrifice.

It is interesting to note that a Jewish Rabbi living today might tell you that when the Messiah comes, He will explain the meaning of every letter. Well, we know the Messiah has come, Jesus, and He gave us the Holy Spirit who will teach us all things (John 14:26) including the meaning of every Hebrew letter.

In Psalms 55:22 the Hebrew word "cast" has three letters: Shin, Lamed, Kaf. With the Holy Spirit as the Teacher, He can show us the meaning of the Hebrew letters. Most scholars agree that each letter can have multiple meanings. This is what the Holy Spirit showed me about them:

Shin – the picture of the letter Shin is that of three fingers like a salute and stands for the Hebrew name of God: Shaddai or Spirit of God, Holy Spirit.

Lamed – the picture of the letter Lamed is that of shepherd's staff and has the idea of learning or teaching.

Kaf – the picture of the letter Kaf is that of the palm of the hand and has the idea of safety, intimacy, and strength.

Putting these letters and their meanings together, we have: God the Holy Spirit teaching (us about) the palm of the hand. To summarize the meaning, Holy Spirit wants to teach us about the importance of God's hand. Therefore, we will look at applicable scriptures about the hand of God:

Psalms 31:15a: My times are in Your hand.

Psalms 63:8: My soul follows close behind You; Your right hand upholds me.

Proverbs 3:16: Length of days is in her (speaking of wisdom) right hand, in her left-hand riches and honor.

John 10:28-30: And I give them eternal life, and they shall never perish; neither shall anyone snatch them out of My hand. My Father, who has given them to Me, is greater than all; and no one is able to snatch them out of My Father's hand. I and My Father are one.

Putting these together, how does this help us define cast or casting? Remember, we are to cast our cares or burdens on Him – why would we do that and how can we trust this is what we are supposed to do?

The Hebrew word for cast tells us to let the Holy Spirit teach us about God's hand. Let us say we are concerned about one of our children. The meaning is we can cast this child into His hand because that is where they are safe or put another way, where the Lord keeps them safe. In God's hand there is eternal life, there is salvation, no one can harm them, no one is able to kill them, no one is able to steal them, no one is able to destroy them.

The alternative is they stay in our hand with us thinking about them, trying to figure out what to do or what is next for them and then when it does not go well, we start the "what if, if only" endless circle (what if I had done this or what if I had done that and then this would not have happened or if only I had said this or not said that, it would be better). We can trust that putting our child in His hand is far better than us holding on to them.

Remember, we believe God is good and that He will not cause or do harm, ever, and because He loves us so, He cares, so much so that He wants to take all your cares and burdens and keep them not just safe in His hand, but at the same time that we cast them into His hand, He begins to save them, to do His work and then we can find rest.

There is a saying that goes, when we rest, God works and when we work, God rests. The meaning is simple: let go of that care by throwing or casting it to the Lord and He will do the work that needs to be done to fix, heal, bring back to the right path, save, and/or finish what He began, all because we take an attitude of rest as we trust Him with the care.

God has got this, and our role is to cast these cares and concerns on Him, over and over again as necessary, until we can rest in His faithfulness knowing that He will handle (hand-le) them, which allows Him to save them and provide peace for us in the midst of the cares and concerns we are so prone to want to carry and that is ALL Good News!

ADDENDUM NOTE 4

This section provides further study on why it is not correct thinking that God allows evil to happen. This study is not definitive; instead, it is more information to help you conclude for yourself that God is a good God that does not allow evil to happen to the believer.

The question goes something like this: "If God is always good, why does He allow evil to happen?" I have spoken to Bible teachers that consider this to be one of those "hard" questions that we cannot answer, at least not easily. They try to explain it by saying something like, "It is hard to explain the ways of the Lord sometimes, but we just have to trust Him anyway." Now, on the surface this looks like a good response, after all, God is God and He can do what He wants, but if we believe God is good all of the time and we believe God causes or allows evil to happen such as the massacre of over six million Jews under Nazi Germany, how can we trust Him to always do good to us – He might just cause or allow something really bad to happen to us.

I am here to tell you that God never causes evil to happen to us, nor does He allow evil to happen in the world that humanity so often attributes to Him as being "an act of God." The more applicable question is, "If God does not allow evil to happen, why does God not stop evil from happening?"

Let us say you have a daughter: would you ever give someone permission to harm her? No, of course not – can you imagine a father saying, "Sure, teach her a lesson that it is dangerous to drive by smashing her car and putting her in the hospital." It is ridiculous just to think it – do you agree? Then why would we project this same way of thinking on God that He would allow this sort of thing to happen?

Okay so if He does not allow or give permission to anyone to cause evil to happen, you might say, "If He is Almighty God, why does He not stop it from coming?"

At this point, Bible teachers like to talk about the "Sovereignty of God" and even something they call "Ultimate Sovereignty" or "Absolute Sovereignty," saying we cannot explain certain events because it is the sovereignty of God, but frankly, not only does it not explain it, but it leads us in circles ultimately back to the same question, "If God is good, why does He allow evil to happen?"

First, we must base our lives and beliefs on scripture, on the Bible. This is the word of God, and we are in danger of wrong believing any time we go outside what the Bible says. Does the word "Sovereignty" or "Sovereign" appear in the original writing of scripture? No, it is not a part of the scripture (if you have a Bible program and search for these words, you may find it in the titles of Psalms, but translators added titles later, and they are not a part of the original writing). Therefore, anything we base on those words is beyond scripture; although, there might be scripture that gives a basis to the meaning of the word.

The definition of sovereignty is, "supreme power, freedom from external control (autonomous), and/or a controlling influence." Now, is God all those definitions and do scriptures substantiate them? Yes, He is the Supreme power who is free from all external control, and He is the ultimate controlling influence. We often refer to a king as a sovereign and we know that Jesus is the King of Kings and therefore, it is easy to conclude that He is sovereign, in the typical use of the word.

The challenge comes when we try to explain the sovereignty of God as a human being, but God is not a human being – He is a divine being with faculties beyond our comprehension. Then you have others that want to take it, as they say, "to the nth degree" by using terms such as "Ultimate Sovereignty" or "Absolute Sovereignty," but let us be clear: God is sovereign that is enough. The simplicity of it and yet the deep vastness of it is that God is a divine being who is sovereign, in the typical use of the word, i.e. He is autonomous with complete freedom.

On the other hand, I am a human being not autonomous, relying on His wonderful work of grace in my life, every moment of every day. All too often I see theologians, ministers, teachers, and pastors that have spent countless hours trying to explain it beyond that which is the scope of the human mind and frankly, what I see all throughout history are false doctrines, even heresies that arise as a result of trying to explain things such as these that are not explainable in human terms apart from the simplicity of He is God and I am human.

Personally, I do not struggle with the sovereignty of God – He is God, and I am not. What I take issue with is someone who tries to use the sovereignty of God to explain why evil happens, using statements such as, "this happened because of the sovereignty of God," thinking that is going to help anyone. Instead, it often leads someone, especially if they had tragedy in their life, to doubt God is good all the time.

Always believe the scriptures: God is good and just because we cannot explain certain things that happen in the world, trust in the Lord and His Word, the Bible, not in what man says.

What can we say then about why God appears as though He does not stop evil from happening? First, God is always at work stopping evil from happening and goes beyond what we are capable of comprehending to work good out of evil. Let me ask you, what can you do as a parent with a teenage daughter to be 100% certain that no harm comes to her? What if you build an underground concrete fortress, complete with electricity, running water, and all that she needs to live – perhaps if you force her to live in that shelter that would keep her safe from all the harm the world could bring, right, but what kind of life is that for her?

If we apply this to our life on earth with God, at the very least, for God to "stop" every evil thing from happening, He will need to make us all robots without freewill to make choices and instead, He will make every decision for us, but what kind of life would that be? That is no life at all!

If we go back to the beginning, we see God gave Adam and Eve all they needed to live a life free from harm and the part that made them human was the ability to choose whether to obey God when He said in Genesis 2:16-17, "And the Lord God commanded the man, saying, 'Of every tree of the garden you may freely eat; but of the tree of the knowledge of good and evil you shall not eat, for in the day that you eat of it you shall surely die'." One day we will understand the vastness of the garden that God created for Adam and Eve to live in with everything they needed and a tremendous amount of liberty where they could freely eat of all that was there except just one tree. This one tree, whether to eat of it was their choice, making them human, but He was clear that death would begin the moment they ate of the tree of the knowledge of good and evil and they did eat it, ushering in death, which we all experience today.

Since that time, even though we, starting with Adam, chose to disobey Him, God has been at work redeeming man, showing His great love and commitment to humanity by working on our behalf to bring us back to the fruit we are supposed to eat: the tree of life. He showed His ultimate commitment when He gave His beloved Son for us, to redeem us and bring us back to walk with Him as Adam did in the garden. However, what we have is better because Adam walked with God beside him, but we walk with God inside us!

The benefit of this is that we have God living inside of us and He always wants to speak to us, guide us, teach us, and show us the way of righteousness. Believing that God is working all things for good to us who believe, God wants us to be righteous or in a "state of what we ought to be," safe from harm (see Psalms 91). He accomplishes this by talking to us, guiding us every moment of the day with advice, and our part is to listen to Him and follow His advice. Would you not do the same for your children?

In addition, if you believe what it says in Psalms 91:10, "No evil shall befall you" and Psalms 91:9, "because you have made the Lord, who is my refuge, even the Most High, your dwelling place," you are giving God permission to protect you even when you do not know you need protecting, and by the way, even if you do not formally give Him permission to protect you, He is always working to keep you from harm anyway!

I have testimonies from my own life where He spoke to me to do this or that, which kept me from harm or kept me from harming others. As a new believer, I believed everything I read in the scripture and did not question or doubt it at all. For instance, when I read that He answers prayer, I believed it – I was 100% persuaded in my heart that no matter what I asked Him for, He would answer it – you might say I was naive, and maybe I was, but I had radical results that even to this day I get excited when I think about them.

Let me tell you one of the results of believing He answers prayer and that He is a good God that wants to give good gifts to His children. Being a new believer was a radical change for me – I passed from a path of death to a path of life that in every way felt like I was a new creation. At the time, I was driving concrete trucks in Houston, TX. These trucks are big, heavy, and dangerous carrying up to 90,000 pounds of concrete such that if the truck hits a car full speed, there is likely to be fatalities. Often, I would drive one of the older trucks that did not have the best brakes, and in fact, when coming up to a stop light, I had to plan way in advance to start stopping or else I would go through the intersection. With us on a deadline to get the concrete to the construction site, we did not want to slow down unless we had to slow down. Something amazing happened when I became a believer: I found that if I asked God, "Do I slow down because the light is about to turn red, or do I keep on trucking because the light is going to stay green?", I knew in my heart when the answer was "keep going" and I knew when it was "stop." How could this be? Was God manipulating the stop lights to stay green so that I did not have to stop? Although He could if He wanted to do so, He is smart enough to know when the light would turn red! It always amazed me when I heard the answer from Him, obeyed it, and saw the results – it made me want to trust Him more.

He wants to do the same for you – I encourage you talk to Him always about anything you need – believe that He is good and as it says in Hebrews 11:6, "But without faith it is impossible to please Him, for he who comes to God must believe that He is, and that He is a rewarder of those who diligently seek Him." He wants to bless you, reward you and as you seek Him, believing He is good, that reward comes and because of grace (unmerited and undeserved favor), it often comes whether you ask for it or not because He is a good God that loves to give His children good gifts.

The truth that sets you free is that every time you ask God to stop evil from happening to you, He stops it and in fact, when you trust in Psalms 91 protection, even when you are not asking directly, arrows or bullets may fly by day, as it says in Psalms 91:5, but you will not be afraid because you are saying, "He is my refuge and my fortress; My God, in Him I will trust."

I have read dozens of stories about people that never made it to the World Trade Center towers the morning of 9/11. All facts indicate that there should have been thousands more in the towers when the tragedy occurred but there are stories of people's alarms not going off, people who never got sick but woke up sick that morning, and delays in the subways. Way before 9/11, we were in a ministry where traveling teachers would come to our location and one of these told us his story where just a few months before coming to our location, he was supposed to get on Pan Am flight

103 that exploded from a terrorist bomb, but the Lord told him not to get on the plane – thankfully he obeyed and lived to tell the story.

Right before the end of World War I, the Prime Minister of England gave charge to one of his commanders, General Allenby, to deliver Jerusalem from the hands of German and Turkish forces as a morale-boosting Christmas present for the British nation. After Allenby secured Jerusalem by defeating the armies that surrounded it, he marched into the city and gave this proclamation: "I make it known to you that every sacred building, monument, holy spot, shrine, traditional site, endowment, pious bequest or customary place of worship, of whatever form of the three religions, will be maintained and protected according to the existing customs and beliefs of those to whose faith they are sacred."

This happened on December 9, 1917, and it was also the first day of Hanukkah. This event was so special to the Jews at the time that they interpreted it as a modern-day Hanukkah miracle. The release of the Balfour Declaration just a month earlier stated that his majesty's government viewed "with favor the establishment in Palestine of a national home for the Jewish people." The result is that Israel was now open for all Jewish people dispersed throughout the world to return, including millions of Jews in Eastern Europe and of course, all Jews in Germany.

This was the goodness of God working favorably toward the Jews to bring them home after 2,000 years of exile. This was God at work showing His on-going love for the nation Israel and this miracle was an open invitation for all the Jews to return home. God was working mightily to bring His people home, but the sad choice made by hundreds of thousands, if not millions of Jews is they did not return home to Israel. There were multiple calls from various Jewish leaders at the time for the Jews to come home, a prophetic voice, if you will, telling them to come back to their origin, but a majority ignored the call, the invitation, from God to return to their land. Fast forward to World War II and we see the tragic result for millions of Jews. God did not allow the evil to punish them; instead, knowing that it was coming, He worked diligently through people and events to bring the Jews back to their homeland and stop the tragedy that was about to happen, but most made the choice not to receive His invitation and come home and yet, God remains at work to keep all His people from harm because He is a good God.

I have been in a near fatal car accident in Mexico; I have been in an airplane that lost cabin pressure filled with jet exhaust; I have been with a group in a third world country that was held up by terrorist; I have fallen off a water fall where at the bottom of the fall was 90% rock; even before I was a believer, I was driving a car, passed out (I am convinced angels were driving me home), brought to consciousness twice to see how fast I was going, and how reckless I was driving, but in this and with all these things, I see a good God who wants me to live and not die, who wants only good things for me and as I trust Him more each day, as it says in Psalms 91:15-16, "He shall call upon Me, and I will answer him; I will be with him in trouble; I will deliver him and honor him. With long life I will satisfy him and show him My salvation" and that is ALL Good News!

Printed in Great Britain
by Amazon

22771239R00050